Living Nembutsu

Rejoicing in the Compassion of the Buddha,
respecting and aiding all sentient beings,
I will work towards the welfare
of society and the world.

Jodo Shinshu Life Principles

Living Nembutsu

Applying Shinran's Radically Engaged Buddhism in Life and Society

Jeff Wilson

Living Nembutsu:
Applying Shinran's Radically Engaged Buddhism in Life and Society
Jeff Wilson

Published by
The Sumeru Press Inc.
PO Box 75, Manotick Main Post Office,
Manotick, ON, Canada K4M 1A2

Cover illustration: Tessa Asato

ISBN 978-1-896559-90-2

LIBRARY AND ARCHIVES CANADA CATALOGUING IN PUBLICATION

Title: Living nembutsu : applying Shinran's radically engaged Buddhism in life and society / Jeff Wilson.
Names: Wilson, Jeff (Lecturer in religious studies), author.
Identifiers: Canadiana 20220472157 | ISBN 9781896559902 (softcover)
Subjects: LCSH: Shinran, 1173-1263. | LCSH: Shin (Sect)—Social aspects. | LCSH: Pure Land Buddhism—Japan.
Classification: LCC BQ8715.4 .W55 2023 | DDC 294.3/926—dc23

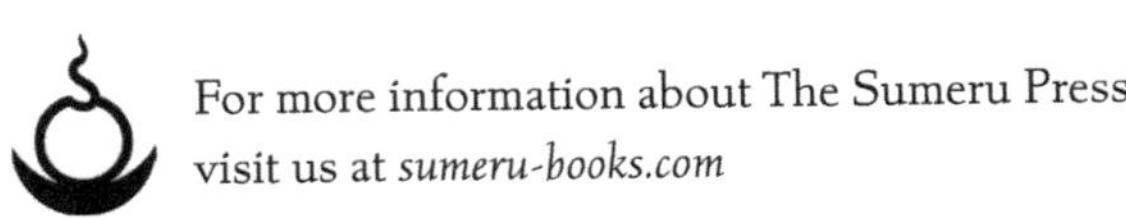
For more information about The Sumeru Press
visit us at *sumeru-books.com*

Contents

Attributions and Gratitude

THIS BOOK ARISES from invited presentations given to various Jodo Shinshu groups since 2003. In particular I thank the Buddhist Churches of America, BCA Eastern Buddhist League, BCA Southern District, Center for Buddhist Education, Hawai'i Island Federation of Buddhist Women's Associations, Honpa Hongwanji Mission of Hawai'i, Jodo Shinshu Buddhist Temples of Canada, Kaua'i Hongwanji Council, Aiea Hongwanji Mission, Buddhist Temple of Chicago, Buddhist Temple of Southern Alberta, Calgary Buddhist Temple, Hamilton Buddhist Temple, Honpa Hongwanji Hilo Betsuin, Manitoba Buddhist Temple, Mo'ili'ili Hongwanji Buddhist Temple, New York Buddhist Church, Orange Country Buddhist Church, San Fernando Valley Hongwanji Buddhist Temple, Seattle Betsuin Buddhist Temple, Toronto Buddhist Church, and Vista Buddhist Temple for providing me with the opportunity to present my ideas and receive community feedback.

Additionally, a version of Chapter 2 was presented to a joint session of the Queer Studies in Religion and Religion and Cities Consultations at the American Academy of Religion annual meeting in 2011; a version of Chapter 4 was presented as the BDK Fujitani Lecture at Chaminade University in 2018; a version of Chapter 5 was presented to the 2021 International Western Dharma Teachers Gathering; and various portions of the manuscript have been included in course lectures at the University of Waterloo—I thank the attendees of all of these presentations for their comments.

Furthermore, I would especially like to thank Bishop Tatsuya Aoki of the Jodo Shinshu Buddhist Temples of Canada, Bishop Marvin Harada of the Buddhist Churches of America, Reverend Patricia Usuki of San Fernando Valley Hongwanji Buddhist Temple, and President Hoshina Seki of the American Buddhist Studies Center for reading the draft manuscript and providing feedback.

Deep thanks to Tessa Asato, artist and member of White River Buddhist Temple, for the use of her remarkable cover art image. Readers interested in Ms. Asato's art can find more at www.tessatoworld.com. Her image wonderfully depicts the multi-generational, diverse and vibrant Jodo Shinshu community. Many people mistakenly think that Pure Land Buddhism is mostly Buddha-centred, due to the importance of Amida Buddha. But actual living Jodo Shinshu in North America and Hawai'i is strongly sangha-centred. It is the sangha of living, breathing, ordinary fellow practitioners that forms the heart and primary orientation of Canadian and American Jodo Shinshu. It is through and with the sangha that we are embraced just as we are, and it is the always-supportive, all-inclusive sangha that provides us with a glimpse of the joy and solidarity of the Pure Land.

Finally, my thanks to John Negru, publisher of Sumeru Books, who took this project on and provided an important outsider's perspective as editor and conversation partner.

Portions of Chapter 2 were published in the *Journal of Global Buddhism* in "All Beings Are Equally Embraced By Amida Buddha: Jodo Shinshu Buddhism and Same-Sex Marriage in the United States," Volume 13 (2012): 31-59, https://www.globalbuddhism.org/article/view/1191.

A portion of Chapter 3 was published in *Buddhadharma: The Practitioner's Quarterly* as "Amida Buddha Welcomes All Refugees," Winter 2019.

An alternate version of Chapter 5 was published in the *Journal of Buddhist Ethics* as "Principles for Jōdo Shinshū Social Engagement," [Volume 29, 2022: 145-175].

A portion of Chapter 6 was published in *Tricycle: The Buddhist Review* as "Born Together With All Beings," Summer 2019.

Most included quotes from Shinran come from Dennis Hirota, Hisao Inagaki, Michio Tokunaga, and Ryushin Uryzu, eds., *The Collected Works of Shinran: Volume I, The Writings*. Jōdo Shinshū Hongwanji-ha, 1997. In some cases, they are slightly modified to conform to the style of this book. Additionally, the hymn on page 48 about Amida Buddha's "saving hands" comes from *Jogai Wasan*, translated by Hisao Inagaki, in *Yamada Meiji Kyōju Kanreki Kinen*

Ronbunshū: Sekai Bunka to Bukkyō, edited by Yamada Meiji, Nagata Bunshōdō, 2000: 20.

The poem by Reverend Mariko Nishiyama on page 15 was originally published in *The Buddhist Wheel* (July 2006) and is used with her permission.

For the sources of ministers' extended blockquotes in Chapter 2, please see my article "All Beings Are Equally Embraced by Amida Buddha" in the 2012 issue of the *Journal of Global Buddhism*.

The excerpt from Chomei's *Account of My Ten Foot Hut* on pages 66-67 comes from Dr. Robert Lawson's translation found at https://www.washburn.edu/reference/bridge24/Hojoki.html.

The blockquotes from Reverend Hozen Seki on pages 120-121 come from *The Great Sound of Enlightenment*, published by the American Buddhist Academy [American Buddhist Study Center], 1989.

The quote from Reverend Kenryu Tsuji on pages 129-131 is from his article "Oso Eko and Genso Eko" in *The Wheel of Dharma*, December 1996.

The quote from Dr. Nobuo Haneda on page 132 comes from his article "What is the Pure Land," found at the website for the Maeda Center of Buddhism (https://maida-center.org/).

The quotes from the *Smaller Pure Land Sutra* on pages 136 and 141 come from Hisao Inagaki's *The Three Pure Land Sutras: A Study and Translation*, Nagata Bunshodo, 1994. The former quote is slightly modified for ease of reading.

The hymn excerpt by Reverend Kenryu Tsuji on page 146 comes from "Gassho to Amida," in *Praising Amida's Virtues: Jōdo Shinshū Service Book*, Honpa Hongwanji Mission of Hawai'i, 2010. The poem excerpt by Rev. Tsuji on pages 146-147 comes from *The Heart of the Buddha-Dharma*, Ekoji Buddhist Temple and Numata Center for Buddhist Translation and Research, 2003.

The poem on page 151 is by Ryōkan, ["When I think"] from *Dewdrops on a Lotus Leaf: Zen Poems of Ryōkan*, translated by John Stevens. Copyright © 1993 by John Stevens. Reprinted by arrangement with The Permissions Company, LLC on behalf of Shambhala Publications Inc., Boulder, Colorado, shambhala.com.

Introduction

Rooted in the Buddha-Ground

> How joyous I am, my heart and mind being rooted in the Buddha-ground of the universal Vow, and my thoughts and feelings flowing within the Dharma-ocean, which is beyond comprehension!

So proclaimed Shinran Shonin as he completed his magnum opus, the *Kyogyoshinsho*, in 1224 CE. Joy flowed out of him despite the years of hardship and persecution he'd endured. From that joy and suffering the Jodo Shinshu movement of Pure Land Buddhism was born, and in the years ahead it spread to every corner of Japan. Along the way Shinran's radical vision of absolute equality—combined with Amida Buddha's first priority of liberating those who suffer the most in society—stimulated a great awakening in the Japanese masses. This in turn led to peasant uprisings that threw off the shackles of the military government and produced semi-democratic self-rule by the peasants and Jodo Shinshu priests of Kaga Province for nearly a century. Since the forced opening of Japan to the outside world in the mid-19th century, Jodo Shinshu has slowly spread to every inhabited continent, nurturing activists, farmers, fishermen, politicians, artists, and office workers alike. That Buddha-soil has indeed proven fertile, and the Dharma-ocean has floated countless ordinary people to awakening.

As we face a new era of extreme climate change, hyper-polarization in politics and society, technological disruption, war, and oppressions of every kind, I find myself reflecting on what seeds may grow from that rich Buddha-soil in which Shinran was rooted. He was a fierce but humble proponent of the common person during a time of intense social chaos and natural disasters, who understood that the way forward could only be found through reliance on the Dharma and solidarity with other suffering people. I can't help but feel that he has something worthwhile to teach us, if we will listen.

Many times, I have encountered Jodo Shinshu Buddhists asking, "What is the relevance of Pure Land Buddhism today?" "How would Shinran respond to movements like Black Lives Matter or the fight for transgender inclusion?" "What is the Jodo Shinshu stance on this or that social issue (abortion, war, euthanasia, capitalism, the environment, policing, the death penalty—and many more)?" There is a hunger for answers. This book doesn't contain them all, because answers are ultimately something we each need to find for ourselves as we re-write Buddhism with our own lives. The directions I point to here won't be satisfying for everyone, which is how it should be. I'm just one person, with limited knowledge, formed by various forces that are only relevant to some. But to respond to the many sincere questions that I keep receiving, here I offer my own opinions and, more importantly, seek to provide some vocabulary and concepts for Jodo Shinshu Buddhists to think with as we struggle to apply Shinran's insights in our tumultuous times.

This book evolved out of talks that I have been giving in Jodo Shinshu temples over the past two decades, in response to invitations to speak on subjects such as immigration, LGBTQ+ rights, climate change, and Buddhist social engagement. Jodo Shinshu readers, who share a common set of references and religious understanding with me—even though many may reach different conclusions about this or that important social issue—will already be familiar with the basic vocabulary of Pure Land Buddhism. But to make it more accessible to readers from other Buddhist traditions or different religions, let's quickly introduce a few topics and terms that occur in the book.

Shinran was a religious genius of the 12th and 13th centuries—he is often called Shinran Shonin, since Shonin is a term of respect for a saintly figure. He practiced Pure Land Buddhism, which is the mainstream form of Buddhism in Japan (partly as a result of his efforts), as well as much of East Asia. His specific school of Pure Land Buddhism is called Jodo Shinshu—sometimes shortened to

Shin in English—which means "True School of the Pure Land," i.e., a Buddhist tradition that faithfully practices the core meaning of the Pure Land way. There is also a closely related school of Pure Land Buddhism founded by Shinran's teacher, Honen, that is called Jodo Shu and is the second largest form of Buddhism in Japan, after Jodo Shinshu. Pure Land Buddhism derives its vision from the story of Amida Buddha, a cosmic figure of unflinching compassion and wisdom who reveals to us the natural unfolding of Dharma (truth/reality) in our lives. As Rev. Mariko Nishiyama poetically put it:

Amida Buddha embraces all life in all forms.
All are integral parts of infinite life:
birds, fish, animals, grass, plants, trees, and yes, even humans.
Nothing is excluded—from the most complex
to the smallest invisible cell.
All awaken to truly live in Amida Buddha's infinite life.
Namo Amida Butsu.

Namo Amida Butsu is a phrase that we recite as our main practice:

Namo (or Namu): literally "I venerate" or "I take refuge," but in the Jodo Shinshu context the meaning is more like "I give thanks."
Amida: literally "Infinite/Boundless," which serves as a contraction for Infinite Light and Boundless Life; these stand for wisdom and compassion, respectively.
Butsu: literally "Buddha," which indicates both an awakened being and the inconceivable liberated reality which awakens us all.

This phrase is called the *nembutsu*: literally, "mindfulness of Buddha." Pure Land Buddhists recite it thankfully at services and throughout the day when we feel the Dharma-ocean flowing through our lives, embracing and supporting us. Those who are particularly awakened to the presence of Great Compassion are said to have received *shinjin*, literally "trusting heart/mind."

One more term to define: Pure Land. This is a multivalent term that relates to Amida Buddha. In the founding story contained in the *Sutra on Immeasurable Life* (often called the *Larger Pure Land Sutra* in English), Amida Buddha establishes the Pure Land as a way for all beings to be freed from suffering. In Shinran's writings, the Pure Land is understood as nirvana, the ultimate emancipation and enlightenment that all forms of Buddhism aim for. In general Japanese tradition, the Pure Land is often seen as a posthumous destination, a blissful rebirth that results in Buddhahood. There are yet further meanings, as there are to other key terms such as Amida Buddha, nembutsu, and shinjin.

I began my journey into the Pure Land way at university back in the mid-1990s, and have been benefitted by so many ministers, teachers, and companions. Today I teach about Buddhism at a university, and, probably to everyone's surprise, have become an ordained Jodo Shinshu minister. All of this is through the care and support that I have received from the Buddhist community. This book is dedicated to all the fellow practitioners who have made it possible, and to all who seek a way to put an end to suffering.

1

Radical Shinran

TO EXPLORE THE THOUGHT of Shinran Shonin, who founded the Jodo Shinshu school of Pure Land Buddhism approximately 800 years ago, I want to begin with a story. Takashi Kenryu Tsuji lived in Kyoto in the years before WWII, studying Buddhism and preparing to enter the Jodo Shinshu Buddhist ministry. Born on a farm in British Columbia, Tsuji was a bit out of his element in Japan, so he looked forward to the comfort of his father's letters from home. At first he read them with excitement, but over time he got used to them and barely cared, as his father—a berry farmer, not an intellectual—seemed to say the same sorts of things over and over. Instead, he would snatch out the cheque that his father always included and throw away the letter, hardly reading it. But one day, he sensed something different about a newly arrived letter. Reading it more closely, he saw that his father had written "Because of my creeping old age, I am having difficulty holding a pen. This may be my last letter to you...."

Tsuji was struck by his father's words. He felt sudden deep pain at how he hadn't appreciated his father's love. All those times his father asked about his health and urged him to study hard, he was really expressing his care and concern for his son. But young Tsuji had just taken him for granted and focused only on his own petty desires.

Tsuji earned his ordination, graduated, and headed home on the last ship to leave for Canada before the war broke out. Shortly after he returned, Japan attacked Pearl Harbor and the British Columbia government ordered all Japanese and Japanese Canadian people to be incarcerated in remote concentration camps; the same injustice was inflicted on people in the United States. Tsuji helped the refugees move, then spent the war years running makeshift camp schools and temples. His father died in 1944, a prisoner in the camps.

For the rest of his life, Tsuji kept that last letter he'd received from his father while in Kyoto and treasured it, re-reading it at times. Whenever he did, it was like he was hearing his father one more time. As he explained many years later when he had become the first North American-born bishop of the Buddhist Churches of America, Tsuji felt his father was "very much living in the words he wrote."

Tsuji used this story to explain his philosophy on writing. As he said, "Words never die. By reading the writing of people long gone we can still identity with their religious feelings, thoughts, and philosophy of life. Thus, we can come to the heart of Shinran Shonin's religious life through his living words. What kind of man was he? Did he have a specific message for me?"

Shinran Shonin died over 750 years ago, yet as Tsuji says, his words are still living, and through them he still speaks. So, when I go to his words and consider them, as Tsuji did before me, what do I find? As a researcher in Japanese Buddhist history, how does Shinran strike me? As a Jodo Shinshu Buddhist, what do I value about Shinran?

Although Shinran honored a lineage of seven great Pure Land masters of the past, the truth is that he went far beyond any previous thinkers in Buddhism. Thus, in lectures and Dharma talks over the past dozen or so years I have referred to him as "radical Shinran." For those of us living so long after Shinran's time, and especially those who've been exposed to Jodo Shinshu for all or much of our lives, it can be hard to appreciate just what a staggeringly radical person Shinran was. He was a great innovator, who was constantly moving Buddhism beyond what it had been, looking for new ways to bring the Dharma to an ever-wider audience. His whole career could be summed up as moving further and going beyond: going beyond monastic celibacy, going beyond elitist interpretations of Buddhism, going beyond traditional understandings of Amida Buddha, nembutsu, and how they operate in our lives.

When I examine Shinran in the context of Japanese religious history, there are seven major elements of his teaching in which Shinran was a radical, either bringing entirely new interpretations into Buddhism or creatively expanding them to such an extent that they went far beyond their earlier versions. First, Shinran taught that Amida is not just a person from the past but is true reality itself reaching out to liberate us. Most previous commentators treated Amida Buddha straightforwardly, as a specific person who reached awakening at a certain time and place. But for Shinran, Amida Buddha was a type of skillful means produced by true reality (called "dharma-body" in the Mahayana Buddhist tradition) for our ordinary, unawakened minds to have something to guide them toward liberation. As Shinran wrote, "Dharma-body as suchness has neither colour nor form; thus, the mind cannot grasp it, nor words describe it. From this oneness was manifested form, called dharma-body as compassionate means." We call this dharma-body of compassionate means Amida Buddha, depict it in statues and paintings, and tell stories about it as our way of encountering suchness and being guided beyond names, forms, and dualistic concepts.

Second, Shinran stated that encountering the Pure Land is not confined to the next life—we experience our first awakening with the arising of shinjin (the trusting heart) during this lifetime, which is then expanded and fulfilled at the end of our present lives. This means that our current lives are affirmed as an important site of awakening, so Jodo Shinshu Buddhists aren't just morbidly sitting around waiting to die. As Shinran puts it, "When foolish beings ever floundering in birth-and-death hear the true and real virtues and realize supreme shinjin through Amida's directing of virtue to them by the power of the Vow, they immediately attain great joy and reach the stage of non-retrogression, so that without being made to sunder their blind passions, they are brought quickly to the realization of great nirvana."

Third, Shinran explained that we immediately become fully awakened upon entering the Pure Land, without any additional centuries of training. Previous scholars had taught that birth in the Pure Land is just the first step, followed by years or eons of further work towards eventual awakening. As Shinran says, "When a person has entered completely into the Pure Land of happiness, they immediately realize the supreme nirvana; they realize the supreme enlightenment." This is because the Pure Land is itself nirvana—it is a way of conceiving and discussing the inconceivable. Thus, there is no need for anxiety about our futures or that of our loved ones, for all enter the great ocean of nirvana at the moment of death.

Fourth, Shinran taught that attainment of buddhahood is immediately followed by return to the unenlightened world to help relieve the sufferings of others. Thus, instead of a sort of heavenly paradise where people spend an eternal vacation, this sets up a model of the Pure Land way that includes enthusiastic, energetic work on behalf of others as the living out of compassion. Shinran teaches, "People, once born in the Pure Land of happiness, then conceive in their hearts the wish to be born in the three realms to teach and guide sentient beings; they then abandon their life in the Pure Land and receive birth in accord with their aspiration. Though they are born into the flames of various births in the three realms, the seed of supreme enlightenment will never rot. Why? Because they are sustained by the good of Amida, the perfectly enlightened."

Fifth, Shinran proclaimed that the Pure Land is for everyone, with no exceptions, and therefore there is no need for monastic celibacy, advanced training, vegetarianism, shaved heads, and so on. In other words, even someone like me is embraced by Amida. The idea that anyone, even those who failed to keep the precepts, could attain awakening through the Pure Land way was already circulating in the community of Shinran's teacher, Honen. But only Shinran put it into actual practice by openly marrying, growing hair, and eating meat and drinking alcohol when the occasion called for it.

Sixth, Shinran insisted that self-oriented efforts play no role in the attainment of buddhahood—it is through the working of power beyond the self (called Other Power in the Pure Land tradition) that our liberation comes about. Shinran expressed this thusly: "because of the true cause—Amida Tathagata's directing of virtue for our going forth—we realize the enlightenment of supreme nirvana." Self-centred striving for nirvana is fruitless. For Shinran, we should relax and allow ourselves to be drawn toward awakening, naturally. Thus, awakening is not something we achieve after lifetimes of strenuous practice—it is a natural process that unfolds in our lives as we open ourselves ever more to the Dharma.

And finally, seventh, Shinran showed that nembutsu—the primary practice of Jodo Shinshu—is not a form of begging. Rather, it's a form of thanksgiving. In other traditions of Pure Land Buddhism, nembutsu was and is used as a sort of prayer or mantra: designed to earn you a place in the Pure Land through piety, creating good karma, purifying your mind, or other means. Shinran completely rejected this approach. As he explained, awakening comes about not by earning it for yourself through efforts that are ultimately ego-tainted—rather, awakening is received through the natural working of Amida Buddha's Primal Vow. When we realize this, we say the nembutsu as a way to express our joy and gratitude at this wondrous gift. Nembutsu isn't instrumental and doesn't get us anything: it's a reply to the arising of the trusting heart. This means that from the Jodo Shinshu point of view, true religion is expressive, not benefit-seeking, and is based on wonder and gratitude.

So that's quite a list. Any one of these ideas would've been enough to get most folks labeled as radical. Shinran's list includes seven major items, and there were many other ways in which he was innovative as well.

It's worth emphasizing that even though he was a radical, this doesn't mean that Shinran simply threw away the tradition. In North America, we tend to think that the new replaces the old, which is abandoned. But that wasn't Shinran's approach. His method was to go beyond the past by revitalizing and exploring new possibilities from within the tradition, not throwing the tradition away. He set a great example that we can look to in our own time.

So, yes, Shinran went beyond the conventional understanding of encounter with the Pure Land: he said that it happens in *this* lifetime, when the trusting heart comes to rely on Other Power. But he also used the traditional motifs of birth occurring after death on a lotus blossoming in the Land of Bliss. He went beyond the limited geographical conception of the Pure Land existing far to the West: he emphasized how Amida's light shines *everywhere* throughout the universe and pointed out that the sutras say Amida's Pure Land is actually not far away. But he also used the traditional language of the Western direction when it suited him. He went beyond the static ideas of the Pure Land as a pleasant resting place: he said that the Pure Land is nirvana itself, and that beings born there immediately return to the world of suffering as hard-working bodhisattvas. Yet he also wrote hymns that extolled the beauty and physical features of the Pure Land, which comforted those who heard them in medieval Japan. He went beyond the narrative of the sutras that say that Dharmakara made vows and then afterwards became Amida Buddha about ten kalpas (eons) ago: Shinran said that in reality it seems that Amida has been a buddha from the primordial past, always present to manifest wisdom and compassion. Yet Shinran also spoke extensively about the meaning and value of the story of Amida's vows and practice.

Perhaps most importantly of all, he went beyond the literal words of the 18th vow, which appear to exclude all imperfect or non-believing people: Shinran reinterpreted them to mean their exact opposite, that all people are included, and in fact Amida embraces the worst of us first. But even though he radically reinterpreted it, he didn't get rid of the exclusion clause—he kept it in there, respectful of the tradition, yet willing to push it in new directions.

To me, this method of Shinran's is very important to note. Shinran was one of the most creative teachers in the history of Buddhism. He initiated a completely new movement in Buddhism, one that transformed Japan. His whole life is a transcript of the effort to go beyond the familiar in the search for something better, truer, and more liberating. But importantly, it was not a way of going beyond that cut its ties to the past or denigrated the wisdom of previous generations. He went beyond by bringing the traditions with him into a new era, where the same concepts and motifs could be illuminated by the light of a new generation. In other words, he valued tradition enough to recognize it as a vital source for creativity and reform. He wasn't attached to either self-aggrandizing radicalism or to close-minded fundamentalism.

So, I find him to be a very inspiring role model as I, a Jodo Shinshu Buddhist of the 21st century, try to grapple with the Dharma and with the world that we have inherited. There is a quote from the poet W.H. Auden that I am reminded of here. Auden wrote: "The words of a dead man / Are modified in the guts of the living." That's what Shinran did: he took the words of dead men, such as Shakyamuni Buddha and the Chinese monk Shandao, and gave them new life for his day. And it is our perpetual task to let the words of Shinran be digested and revitalized through our own visceral life experience. It is in this way that we are most faithful to Shinran as our guide. To follow in the footsteps of a radical we must be willing to think and act boldly, adapting to meet the needs of each situation, generation, and culture.

Buddhism of We-ness

Let's turn now to that radical idea at the heart of Shakyamuni Buddha's teaching, the idea of no-self. We see it modified by Shinran in his constant urging for us to go beyond self-power. Buddhism can be summed up as the realization that I am not the centre of the universe, and that when I act like I am, I cause trouble for myself and others. The self—at least in the ordinary way we understand it—is said by the Buddha to basically be a cognitive mistake. For this reason, we can say that Shinran had a very inspiring model himself, for few people have been so revolutionary as Shakyamuni Buddha. The idea of no-self at first seems to contradict our entire experience of our reality. We want to believe that we have some sort of permanent identity, and we struggle in vain to fulfill all the endless desires of this self and protect it from ever coming to any harm. I want to think "I am me. I am Jeff Wilson, and no one else is. The fact that I am Jeff Wilson is the most important truth about life." The fact that I stubbed my little toe occupies more of my thinking than the war going on elsewhere.

We spend time and trouble trying to protect our identities. If anyone says something bad about us, we get angry, and if anything goes wrong, we look around for someone else to blame. We think our identities are very precious and real. But the irony is that we ourselves are the source of most of our own suffering. None of us is free from greed, anger, and ignorance, not even the highest lama or the wisest Zen master, and certainly not me. I am attached to this short, pudgy body, to this name Jeff Wilson, to this identity of myself as a specific person living in Canada. When I let those attachments blind me to how much I rely on the help and support of others, that's when the trouble really starts.

I think of an incident that happened when we visited with my in-laws for Christmas. My wife's mom had two little girls from her second marriage. The girls are a few years apart, and they were at an age where they constantly got on each other's nerves. They were fighting every day we were there, and it got to the point where the older one wished out loud that her little sister didn't live with them. I looked on smugly while all of this was going on and thought that they should just get over it. I observed how attached they were to very petty issues that really came down to one sister asserting her ego against the other, all while the parents and other family members were working their tails off to give both girls a safe, happy life and a bunch of presents for the holidays. They should just drop their self-centredness and be grateful for what they have, I thought, patting myself on the back for being such a good Buddhist all the while.

So of course, I was creating a lot of self-righteous karma by focusing on my own understanding, my own power to allegedly transcend the problems of human relationships. Sure enough, I got my come-uppance a few days later. My wife and I had a private guest bedroom in the basement all to ourselves the first couple of weeks we were there. Then two more guests came to town, and we had to move upstairs to use the older sister's bedroom instead. I was very put out: the upstairs bed wasn't quite as comfortable, and the room wasn't quite as private. I spent the whole rest of our vacation mentally grumbling at the new guests for coming and dislodging us. I certainly didn't think to appreciate their presence or understand their right to be there too. Worse yet, the new guests were elderly ladies who had just arrived, whereas I was a young person who had been there for weeks and probably worn out my welcome. And I was only able to be there in the first place because my in-laws had been very welcoming to us with their already crowded house. But did I think about that? I can promise you, I did not. Turns out that when it came down to it, I was just as blind to my foolish self-centredness as my sisters-in-law. Except it was a lot worse in my case, because I was an adult, and I'd gone around on my high horse thinking I could diagnose their problems and prescribe the solution.

All this grumbling and misery was purely due to my self-centred mentality. Shinran always urges us to go beyond self-centredness, to go beyond the egocentricity that imagines itself as uniquely important and capable of solving all its own problems. Although we've heard this idea before in our temples, I think we get used to it and forget just how radical a notion this really is. One way we can understand Shinran is to see that he was a great revolutionary who went beyond not only the understanding of other Buddhists in 13th century Japan, but also actually took Buddhism beyond all its former orientations to create a new Buddhism designed to liberate all people, no matter how good or how bad. The way to recognize this is to see that Buddhism has basically progressed through three major stages of understanding and orientation. I call them "I, they, and we."

In the earliest stage, Buddhism was focused on individual liberation: *I* will detach myself; *I* will perfect my mind; *I* will achieve nirvana. The saint who reached this stage was called an *arhat*, meaning "worthy one," and when they died, they passed away completely, leaving the world behind to continue its struggles for relief from suffering. The arhat had compassion for others, of course, but above all else, this form of Buddhism valued wisdom, the quality which saw through the falsehoods of the ego and heroically seized the truth. This was Buddhism with what I call an I-orientation.

The next stage in Buddhism was the evolution of the bodhisattva ideal, where the saint sought to achieve a high level of spirituality to share the fruits of liberation with others. The bodhisattva took oaths, vowing: *they* need help and I will become their savior; *they* are deluded and I will enlighten them; *they* will all be buddhas when I am done. The bodhisattvas, meaning "enlightening beings," returned again and again to the suffering world to help others achieve the level that they had reached. This form of Buddhism included the wisdom of emptiness, but it especially valued compassion, the others-focused value that drove the personal quest for buddhahood in order to be of assistance to the rest of us. I call this Buddhism with a they-orientation.

The third stage of Buddhism was initiated by Shinran. It collapses the distance between the savior and the saved, declaring that all people are ultimately incapable, and all people are already embraced by wisdom and compassion. Shinran's equation always includes himself along with everyone else: *we* are foolish, *we* are suffering, *we* are embraced just as we are. There are no saints in this formula, only *bonbus*, meaning "ordinary people," saying the nembutsu together and joining the Pure Land together. Therefore, this is a Buddhism that values gratitude, the sense of affection and humility that arises when we realize that I and they are inseparably interconnected as *we*. Thus, we say the nembutsu in thankfulness, not as a prayer for our salvation but as a tribute to the love and support that is given to us all, and for the inner togetherness that we share with one another and all things. I call this Buddhism with a we-orientation.

You can see a nice example of this in the current service book of the Buddhist Churches of America, the largest Jodo Shinshu organization outside of Japan. In traditional Buddhism, the three refuges are very simple. They're just *Buddham saranam gacchami, Dhamman saranam gacchami, Sangham saranam gacchami.* I take refuge in the Buddha, I take refuge in the Dharma, I take refuge in the Sangha. But as we say them in the Buddhist Churches of America, there is a twist. We say: "I take refuge in the Buddha. May *we, together with all sentient beings*, awaken to the Great Way of Enlightenment and to the unsurpassed intent of Amida Buddha. I take refuge in the Dharma. May *we, together with all sentient beings*, enter the storehouse of the Dharma, becoming like the Wisdom Ocean. I take refuge in the Sangha. May *we, together with all beings*, become units in true accord, in harmony with *all* things." So built in right there is a transformation from an I to a we perspective, that embraces and is embraced by all things.

These are the three stages of Buddhism, as I see it: I-they-we. There is nobility in each stage, and we can learn much from studying a wide range of Buddhist schools. People aren't all the same, and the type of Buddhism that works for one person may not always be suited for someone else, with their unique karma, personality, and circumstances. But for me as a practitioner, it is Shinran's vision that I find most compelling, and which most accords with my own experiences. And in such an individualistic culture as ours, there is something radical in the simple notion of focusing on the community, rather than your own ego.

I saw a dramatic demonstration of inner togetherness a few years ago. Hiroshima is a traditional stronghold of Jodo Shinshu, with many very devout Nishi Honganji (the largest branch of Jodo Shinshu) families. Thirty thousand practitioners in Hiroshima submitted pictures of themselves with their palms placed respectfully together, in the position we call *gassho*. Then they took these photos and used them like tiles in a mosaic to create a gigantic image of Amida Buddha. I was very impressed by this innovative form of art. Not only was it highly interesting to look at, it also directly taught the truth of interconnectedness: all of us are knit together with one another whether or not we are able to perceive it. And all of us are the objects of limitless wisdom and compassion embracing us just as we are. Giving up on self-power, we don't simply cease to exist—instead, we discover ourselves participating in a far grander, more beautiful reality than the one projected onto the world by our egocentric attachments.

A Religion of Fearlessness

This vision of a grander, more beautiful, more interconnected, and more mutually supporting reality seems very important today. There are serious challenges facing our world and ourselves as individuals. But at the same time, I feel like there's an excess of negativity in the world. Specifically, I worry about the incredible amount of fear that grips our society.

A lot of times, we're being told to be afraid, not because people are trying to be helpful to us but because they are trying to profit from our fear. They tell us to be afraid of aging and then sell us a skin cream to remove wrinkles. They tell us to be afraid of illness and then sell us expensive medicines. They tell us to be afraid of immigrants, or Muslims, or Mexicans, or Black people, and then tell us that they'll protect us if we'll give them power. They tell us to be afraid of the other political party and then insist that we vote for themselves. Fear isn't just a commonsense caution anymore; it's a whole industry designed to control and exploit us. How often does the news lead off with an uplifting story, or ever report: "things are fine, nothing is going on, there is no news today." The Internet in particular often seems to be just one giant fear and anger machine. The effects on our society, politics, and psyches are deeply damaging and dangerous.

In such an environment, I think that religion should act as a counterbalance against excessive fear and worry. But what do we find when we turn to religion? Many of the religions that are most vocal in the public sphere are busy playing the fear game too, telling us we better do and believe exactly what they say or else we'll suffer a fate far worse than wrinkles, illness, and bad politics. Some go as far as to demand that you believe in Jesus Christ as your lord and savior, or you're going to roast in Hell for eternity, as I got told on the schoolyard as a non-Christian kid. There are attitudes just as divisive and fearmongering in other religions too.

We even find it in Buddhism in several ways. Right action is part of the fundamental Buddhist path, and we should do our best to put the moral advice of the Buddha into action. But some try to force others to act one way or another by scaring them about karma and punishment. For example, in Thailand I visited a temple that had a large sculpture park. The theme of the park was the karmic punishments in the hell realms. They had life-size statues of people being tortured by animal-headed demons, being forced to climb up trees covered in spikes, and all sorts of gruesome things that I won't describe. Let me tell you, it was as bad as a modern-day R-rated horror film. This Hell Park was very popular, and the number one customers who came were school groups. Teachers and parents would always bring large groups of children to come and see the terrible, bloody tortures caused by bad karma, and use it to frighten the kids into obeying their parents and not breaking the law.

Another way that Buddhists have often used fear is to make money from others. For example, hell beliefs have been very important in Japan too. Until the 1980s, the Soto Zen school used to teach that all women are sinful and that they are reborn in hell into a pool of boiling menstrual blood, where they suffer terribly. The only way to avoid this fate was to pay the Zen priests to do a Blood-Pool Hell ritual that would free you or your mother from your bad karma.

On a less dramatic, but even more profitable, scale, this sort of thing is very common in modern Japan. At most temples, you will find them selling *omamori*, which are magic amulets to ward off bad luck. Some temples in the Zen, Nichiren, Shingon, and other traditions make a significant part of their yearly budget from these lucky charms. They have ones for every kind of fear that the Japanese have. There are omamori to prevent a bad grade on a test, to prevent car accidents and plane crashes, to prevent illness, to prevent injury to your children, and so on.

One of the most popular trends is marketing charms to elderly people in Japan, who are told to be afraid of getting old and dying. So, there are Buddhist pillowcases that you can buy: they have been blessed by Kannon Bodhisattva, and when you lie on one at night, it will prevent you from going senile. And there are special Buddhist underwear you can buy too: they've been blessed by the monks so when you wear a pair, you won't experience incontinence. I'm sure it's only a matter of time before they start marketing Buddhist charms to prevent erectile dysfunction. One extremely successful new trend is temples dedicated to easy deaths: you pay the priest and he prays that you'll die suddenly in your sleep. That's right: you're paying him to pray that you will die. Of course, none of these magical practices actually work, and Jodo Shinshu is the only tradition in Japan that rejects them all.

My point here is that like political ideologies, media, and capitalism in general, religion—including Buddhism—is very often involved in exploiting our fears, sometimes supposedly for our own good, sometimes to make money and control us. And it's to this fear-ridden situation, both in general society and in religion, which I think Shinran has something to offer for us in the contemporary world.

As usual, Shinran is a radical. He takes the old way of thinking and turns it around. Shinran says that people of the nembutsu are protected by Amida and by all the powers in the universe. For example, when we chant the *Shoshinge*, the central liturgy of Jodo Shinshu, we say "The light of compassion that grasps us illumines and protects us always." Shinran puts it even more eloquently in the *Kyogyoshinsho* when he says that ordinary nembutsu practitioners are "constantly illumined by the light of the Buddha's heart, grasped and protected, never to be abandoned." Throughout his writings, Shinran constantly assures people that they have nothing to fear because they are watched over by benevolent forces. Among those he lists are Amida, Shakyamuni, Kannon, Daiseishi Bodhisattva, all the Buddhas of the universe, all the gods of heaven and earth, the four Dharma protector deity-kings, dragons, and even evil spirits. He says that even Mara, the Buddhist version of the devil, has been converted to Buddhism and protects people instead of tormenting them.

The point isn't really about invisible protectors, though—it's that we needn't fear the invisible dangers that play such a prominent role in so many religions. We can set aside the common anxieties over supernatural danger and focus on what really matters.

Throughout Buddhist history, including in Japan, monks have accepted donations to pacify or exorcise dangerous spirits. Maybe we could say that Buddhist monks are the original Ghostbusters. The nembutsu was used in this way too before Shinran came along, as a way to ward off ghosts and demons. People would chant Namo Amida Butsu as a type of protective spell to scare away phantoms and goblins. The ancient Japanese believed they lived in a world of spirits and *kami*, and that they had to constantly be on their guard. The elite Buddhist institutions like Mt. Hiei and Koyasan often exploited these fears to keep the masses in line and to gather donations—in fact, the gigantic monastic complex of Enryakuji on Mt. Hiei where Shinran practiced was founded to protect Kyoto from the supposed bad luck that came from the Northeast, and the monks were paid by the government to pray for the ruling powers.

But after Shinran came down from Mt. Hiei and started the Jodo Shinshu movement, he completely threw out all practices designed to protect people from spirits or bad luck, because they were unnecessary. To live in the nembutsu is to already be protected. We can move away from fear and anxiety toward compassion and reflection instead.

There's something very special going on here with Shinran that I want to point out. Unlike in many religions, he doesn't fill people with fear. He never says that we should be afraid of Amida. We don't tell our kids that they better eat all their veggies or else Amida will get them.

Other people are supposed to love God but are also told to be afraid of God. A Roman Catholic friend of mine told me that "God is a jealous God," and it's said that "fear of God is the beginning of wisdom," which some take literally as a commandment to be afraid of a dangerous, potentially wrathful deity. That's an attitude I've never been able to understand. How can you fully love someone who threatens to hurt you, or damn you, or even to annihilate you? It just doesn't seem possible to me. And how could something really be God if it possessed such petty, mean-spirited emotions as jealousy and offended anger? Thankfully, there are less-problematic ideas of godhood out there, but nevertheless many people worship jealous, small-minded versions of divinity, and struggle with the spiritual task of both loving and living in fear of their deity or deities.

Meanwhile, this is an attitude that we fundamentally don't have to live with in Jodo Shinshu. According to Shinran, Amida only always embraces all beings, no matter who they are. That's a very special message. We never say "Amida is a jealous Buddha" or "Fear of Amida is the beginning of wisdom." These sentences sound absurd, even humorous, because they are so completely alien to the Shin tradition. And furthermore, Shinran says that we shouldn't be worried about our afterlife, because it's taken care of by Amida. In fact, in *Tannisho*, Shinran says that he isn't concerned about whether the nembutsu will lead him to the Pure Land or to Hell: he just completely trusts in Other Power and relaxes into his own natural state of being.

Of course, Shinran elsewhere emphasizes that indeed all beings will be born in the Pure Land through the assistance of Amida. The point here isn't about beliefs, it's about attitudes. You may or may not believe that Amida literally protects people from harm or that ghosts exist. These aren't really so important (if ghosts exist, then as a nembutsu practitioner you're protected; if they don't, then there's nothing to worry about in the first place). What is important is to notice that the nembutsu teaching created by Shinran was designed to function in a way that relieved everyday people of their fear and anxiety, instead of trying to make money or converts from it.

Shinran also says that we don't have to be afraid of bad karma. Even if our passions and delusions overwhelm us and we can't help committing some sort of wrong action, we are still embraced and delivered from hellish consequences. As Shinran puts it, when polluted streams enter the vastness of the ocean, they are all purified and transformed into the essence of enlightenment. All of this means that because of Shinran's insight, Jodo Shinshu is one of the very few religions in the world that is not based on fear. There is no fear of an angry deity or a terrible afterlife or a suffering rebirth. For someone like myself who makes many mistakes in life and is fundamentally incapable of earning enough merit to offset my karmic debts, that's a very valuable message to hear.

Because, at least in its ideal form, there is no superstition or fear of judgment in Shin Buddhism, there is much less economic opportunity for exploitation than is often found in religion. We don't have to go to confession; nor do we have anything like the televangelists who swear that if you'll just show your love of God by sending in money, then heaven will reward you with prosperity. We don't have to pay priests to keep us safe from ghosts or demons. We have funeral and memorial services, but they're to comfort the living and remember those we love, not to enable the deceased to go to the Pure Land. Amida has already embraced them, and we have nothing to worry about. Therefore, if we are too poor or otherwise unable to hold a memorial, it doesn't matter whatsoever. Also, we aren't required to pay for all the expensive extra paraphernalia around funeral services and tombstones that you see in other forms of Buddhism. Of course, this also means that we can only raise funds based on people's goodwill and thankfulness. Some other churches raise massive funds by promising that donations will help you to avoid going to Hell or ensure that God smiles on you—and such tactics are hardly absent from many forms of Buddhism, for that matter. But in Jodo Shinshu we don't play on people's fears or greed in that way.

Shinran: A Role Model

There are other implications of Shinran's radical approach to religion. Shinran said that we don't need to do anything in order to earn a spot in the Pure Land. In fact, he said that if we egotistically try to become saints or buddhas then we will fail, because self-attachment is the source of troubles according to Buddhism. Instead, Shinran implored us to let go of self-clinging and trust in power-beyond-self. Whereas our limited efforts may fail, Other Power never fails to bring us to the fulfillment of the Buddhist path. Therefore, we don't need to be afraid of our negative personality traits or limitations. All our personal failings are taken in by Amida and transformed into the wisdom of enlightenment. So, our bad aspects don't hold us back.

This is such a wonderful gift. We may be lazy, or slow-witted, or hyperactive, or judgmental. It doesn't matter—these things won't prevent us from receiving liberation too. We are embraced, warts and all. Therefore, there's no need for anxiety in Jodo Shinshu. We can just relax and say the nembutsu in gratitude. This is why Rennyo—a descendant of Shinran and one of Jodo Shinshu's most important historical leaders—talked about shinjin as *anjin*, the peaceful heart. Those who have awakened to the grasp of Amida are at peace, without fear and anxiety. Sure, they may have difficult times in their lives, but fundamentally they know that they are enveloped by great compassion, and every day is another chance to recognize all that we receive and say thank you. This peaceful heart is a very special gift that we receive from the Shin tradition.

The flip side of this is that if there is nothing we need to do to get into the Pure Land, then we are enabled to try our best without fear of failure. Buddhism has moral guidelines, and we should try to live by them. I certainly do try, though I don't always succeed. Even just the very first precept—do not harm other beings—is very difficult to fulfill. So, if you try to live a moral life, but ultimately you can't help the fact that when you drive at night, your car kills bugs, or maybe you just can't seem to give up your attachment to fried chicken, then it's still alright. You don't have to be perfect in Jodo Shinshu, which gives us permission to simply try to be our best, whatever that means for each of us as individuals. If you're not very good at meditation or can't remember all the steps in the Noble Eightfold Path, or don't really understand what emptiness means, it's OK. To the extent that we live as good Buddhists, our lives and the lives of those around us will be enriched and benefitted. To the extent that we fail to live as perfect Buddhas, we will be drawn on by Other Power and still enter the Pure Land together.

In religion, Shinran is my main guide and role model. When I think of him, I think of a man who was deeply in touch with reality, and who was brave in his beliefs. In the *Kyogyoshinsho* he points out that "fearlessness" is one of the names of nirvana. He was a person who was willing to speak truth to power, as the saying goes. He had the strength to stick to his unpopular views that Amida embraced everyone, even the poor and illiterate. He went into exile, and he even criticized the emperor himself. In 13th century Japan, that was some serious chutzpah! He was truly fearless, but he wasn't a jerk about it. The Pure Land way gave him not only comfort but also courage, and he did what he felt was right, helping others even when he knew there would be a cost to himself.

For those of us who practice Buddhism, I think we can take a lesson here for ourselves. We live in a non-Buddhist culture. Things aren't nearly as bad now as they used to be but we're still a minority, and we can run into problems. When I lived in Hawai'i my landlords were evangelical Christians, and I was so nervous about them that I actually hid our *butsudan* (home altar) when they came in to make some repairs. This wasn't just paranoia. When I lived in North Carolina with my grandmother, her assistant went upstairs one day and found our butsudan. She came down white as a sheet and told my grandmother that there was "something awful" upstairs. Misunderstanding and distrust of Buddhists is still common, even though overt religious discrimination has ebbed.

More to the point, we ourselves can be the problem. We may

not talk about Buddhism with others because we may be afraid that they will reject us. Or we may be afraid that we won't be able to explain Jodo Shinshu very well and be embarrassed. In that case, the mere fear that someone might ask a question that we don't immediately know the answer to is keeping us from even telling someone anything about Buddhism at all. In such situations, I hope we can think of Shinran's example, and take heart. The difficulties we face in telling others about Jodo Shinshu are nothing compared to the ones he faced, and yet he was able to endure hardship and cause the nembutsu to flourish throughout Japan, to the benefit of countless millions. Eight hundred years later, the efforts he made are still paying off all the way here in North America. So too, the challenges that the early generations of Japanese immigrants faced in being Buddhist make our own difficulties look very small. So let us put away fear and go forward boldly with courage instead, with Shinran as our role model.

If Shinran's radical Buddhism is the religion of "no worries," then that's a message we can apply in our own lives and seek to tell others about. For ourselves, I think about something I read in an essay published by the Hongwanji International Center. It said, "Through the Nembutsu we discover a way to live our life to the utmost, with appreciation for the splendors of life." That really captures the spirit of Jodo Shinshu. We are given a way to live our life to the utmost, without fear and anxiety. All that energy which might have been taken up with fear and worry is used instead for appreciating the splendors of life. How marvelous!

In my opinion, we should make this message available to others. If we look outside the temple, we'll find many kinds of people. Among others, one common type comprises those who believe that religion must involve terror and anxiety in the face of an angry, dangerous God (indeed, some believe that morality is impossible without basing it on fear of divine judgment and punishment). Another type that's increasing in numbers comprises those who feel that religion is only a con game left over from an earlier, ignorant age, designed to frighten people into submission (we can easily see how the first group helps provoke the second one). For those locked into one or the other viewpoint, all of us who don't belong to their perspective are deluded and possibly threatening. This results in conflict, and often makes discussion of religion in North America rather shallow, as these combating groups prevent nuanced conversation from emerging. Both these groups can benefit from exposure to Jodo Shinshu, which shows that authentic religion can flourish without fear and worry, and that religion can enhance life in a stressful, materialistic culture that lacks appreciation of the great fortune we experience in North America and the sacrifices that have been made to support our lifestyles. These people don't necessarily need to become Buddhist. We can benefit them simply by showing that their assumptions are wrong, that there are healthier ways to pursue religion that aren't based on fear or exploitation.

I'm reminded of a story from *Essays in Idleness*, a 13th century text that's still popular in Japan. One day a man was walking through the temple district in eastern Kyoto, and he happened to overtake an old, bent-over woman walking along the same path. With every step she said "*kushami*" with great intensity. "Kushami" is the word for a sneeze. The man thought this behaviour was quite odd, so he asked her why she kept saying it. But she didn't reply, she just kept on saying "kushami, kushami." So, he asked her again, but she still ignored him. He tried one more time. Finally, with a look of great annoyance she turned and said to him, "I am the former wet nurse for the crown prince. Don't you know that if someone sneezes, they will drop dead, unless somebody says the magic word 'kushami?' Right now, his highness may be sneezing, and you are preventing me from saving his life!" So saying, she turned away and went on chanting "kushami, kushami, kushami" until she disappeared in the distance.

This lady was trapped in a perpetual state of fear. Because of her fear and superstition, she was forced to say "kushami, kushami" every moment of her life, just in case the crown prince happened to sneeze. She was probably afraid to sleep or eat, in case that prevented her from saying the magic word right at the necessary moment. What a terrible way to live!

This is the kind of life that Shinran frees us from. In Jodo Shinshu, the religion of fearlessness, we are given the gift of a peaceful heart and a mind free from religious anxiety. We are provided with a religious path that can't be exploited for financial gain. Unlike mindfulness meditation, yoga, or other elements of religion, it is impossible to turn the nembutsu into a commodity. Therefore, at its heart Jodo Shinshu practice always lies fundamentally outside the traps of capitalism and marketized spirituality. In this way, we can see that Shin is not just another old Japanese religion, but an actual revolution in human religious history, and one that is as relevant today as it was in the past, if not even more so.

This emphasis on the heart and feeling points back to that list of ways in which Shinran is most truly radical. Unlike all other previous Buddhist thinkers, Shinran says that we chant to express our gratitude at being liberated, not to achieve liberation, generate good karma, or receive magical benefits. For Shinran, nembutsu that is true and real is only an offering of thanks. It isn't begging to get into the Pure Land. It isn't asking for favours, such as a better life or a new car. Nembutsu is saying "Thank you for this life that I have received. Thank you for the boundless light that surrounds me always. Thank you for embracing even such an unworthy person as myself. Thank you for including all beings in collective liberation." That's all it does, because everything else has already ultimately been taken care of for us.

Shinran turns away from the rest of Buddhism and basically says, "You don't have to do anything. You don't have to become something. You just have to be who you are and let yourself be carried beyond your self." Of course, while this sounds simple, Shinran said this was actually the hardest thing of all to do. The self always wants to assert itself, even in the effort to get rid of itself. Trusting oneself to power beyond the self is radically humbling and seems to go against our every impulse. Thankfully, I have Shinran who provides me with the model that this is possible.

To summarize, Shinran introduced many radical ideas into Buddhism, by taking Buddhist tradition and reinterpreting it, or building on it to extend ideas that had never reached their fullest potential. This also had radical implications for how Buddhism could be structured, who could be liberated by Buddhist practice, and how Buddhism would or would not be used to control or exploit ordinary people.

Shinran's way is the way of a radical who holds on to tradition while grasping the changing needs of the present, so that the tradition is given new life and can help us to express our gratitude in the here and now. As society changes and we question the role of Buddhism, I think this is a very useful example to keep in mind.

2
Queer Shinran

Shinran's Buddhism was meant for everyone, but especially for those who were rejected by society and felt to be deeply evil (either by society or themselves), such that their worth and future Buddhahood were very much in doubt. Arguably, no group has been more stigmatized and oppressed than sexual minorities—that is to say, people with same-sex attraction, transgender or nonbinary identities, and others who fall outside strictly proscribed male/female dualities or heterosexual norms. Therefore, it's imperative that we examine the Jodo Shinshu tradition in relation to lesbians, gay men, transgender folks, and other queer persons.

I want to begin by explaining my use of the term "queer." Depending on one's generation, this word can have different meanings or connotations. For some, it has a negative feeling, as it was often used as a slur. I do not use it pejoratively, and I hope readers who have had it used against them as a term of abuse will understand my intentions. For people of my generation and social circles, queer was a reclaimed term of pride, solidarity, and political organization. Ultimately, I intend my use of the word queer to be understood in the most inclusive, welcoming, and non-pejorative way possible.

Especially, I use it here as a technical term derived from Queer Studies, a branch of academic research that has been around for approximately thirty years. In keeping with this tradition of inquiry, I use queer to indicate persons, groups, or ideas that don't fit into dominant notions (especially of sex, gender, and relationships) in a society, and that therefore call those dominant modes into question. Queer is thus both an adjective and a verb: we have queer (LGBTQ+) people, and such people may queer unexamined ideas about sex, gender, and so on by forcing us to reevaluate received wisdom. As such, LGBTQ+ people and communities, in addition to being worthy individuals and subcultures in their own right, provide invaluable service to Buddhism and the larger society by provoking thought, critical self-examination, and transformation.

One more note: although I am writing about Buddhism and LGBTQ+ issues, I do not claim a queer identity for myself. By mainstream standards I am considered straight and gender-conforming. My immediate family has queer people in the previous generation, my generation, and the next generation, and I grew up in a religious environment that accepted gay and transgender people for who they were. Thus, I have been privileged to live around and with LGBTQ+ people, but do not speak from within or for that community myself.

Buddhism and Sexuality

Before I discuss Shinran and queerness specifically, it's necessary to take a short tour through the history of Buddhism and sexuality. Classic Buddhism revolves around a fundamental dualism, which is based primarily on sexuality. On the one hand you have the monastics, who constitute a semi-separate society of sexless ritual practitioners. Whether on mountaintops or in urban temples, they are set apart by particular costumes, rules, and behaviours. On the other hand are the householders, the regular people engaged in sex, work, and other entanglements. While never fully realized as ideal types (monks performed various types of labour, while some householders practiced degrees of renunciative asceticism), these two groups operated as a dyad, with each dependent on the other while enacting degrees of formal separation. The fundamental cleavage between them was celibacy, and this sex-based separation was the basis of both Buddhist religious practice and Buddhist social organization. While Buddhist societies were certainly patriarchal and heterosexist, celibacy/non-celibacy was the most fundamental Buddhist social organizing principle, even more than gender or heterosexualism, and the most distinctive mark of Buddhist cultures in comparison to most others.

For the monastic orders, sexuality was primarily regulated by monastic codes of behaviour. Indeed, monks and nuns lived according to hundreds of rules that governed behaviour in all realms, including sexuality. For monk and nuns, all sexuality was forbidden. They were supposed to be a separate class working to disentangle themselves from delusion and ordinary attachments. Furthermore, sex causes problems in monasteries (just like in regular life) and quickly leads to attachment, greed, anger, and other threats to harmonious communal living. Whether directed toward opposite-sex or same-sex partners, sexual behaviour was treated in an equal manner: don't do it. There was no harsher punishment in the monastic codes for same-sex behaviours compared to opposite-sex activities.

As for sexuality outside of the monasteries, for householders it wasn't nearly as minutely regulated in Buddhist codes, and same-sex behaviours are rarely referenced. Where they were regulated, it was by civil law, not codified in religious laws.

Beyond sexual behaviour, there is a need to talk about gender specifically. Ancient Indian Buddhists recognized between three and five genders. The three constants were male, female, and queer; additionally, some recognized a fourth gender of intersex persons, while some others split the queer category into those who are naturally queer and those who become queer, along with the categories of male, female, and intersex (here I am condensing what is actually a very complicated situation: I recommend Jose Cabezon's book *Sexuality in Classical South Asian Buddhism* to those who really wish to dig into the subject). Male and female were relatively stable, but who belonged to the queer gender and why varied. This category tended to expand over time to encompass a wider cross section of people who didn't conform to mainstream male or female gender norms.

Just because Buddhist societies put little effort into suppressing queer people and recognized the reality of multiple possible gender constructions and identities, we shouldn't therefore automatically assume that they were devoid of prejudice and oppression. Classic Buddhism was thoroughly male supremacist. Gender wasn't a neutral fact of biology or psychology—rather, it represented a hierarchy of moral value. Heterosexual men were allegedly born as men because of their greater moral behaviour in the past, while Buddhist thought held that those born as women had conducted themselves less morally in previous lives. At the bottom of the karmic and social hierarchy were the various categories of queer people, who supposedly landed there due to inauspicious behaviour in the past. In this social order men could become monks, women could become nuns but had to obey the monks, and most queer people couldn't ordain at all. There were exceptions: for instance, if a man transitioned into a woman, it wasn't a big deal—she just had to switch to the nuns' order. They weren't seen as a threat because there was still a "proper" gender category to place them in.

At the same time, although they were in the lowest status category, because they were real legitimate genders, there were possible benefits to the recognition of queerness. Buddhist sources affirmed that all beings had existed in every gender role during their ceaseless cycle through the round of rebirths. Furthermore, Mahayana sutras claimed that bodhisattvas intentionally took on female and various queer forms to liberate beings. This seems to short-circuit attempts to associate holiness only with masculinity. So, while most Buddhists of all traditions believed the exclusion of most queer people from the monastic sangha was justified, violence or other forms of persecution toward queer persons was absolutely not permissible.

One of the more interesting moments of cultural encounter is the story of how Buddhism queered China. When the Indian Buddhist religion arrived in China, it was seen as sexually deviant and socially dangerous by conservative forces; that is to say, it seemed queer. Confucian social structure only allowed for a family-based model of sexuality and social arrangement. With their celibate monastic orders, Buddhists were attacked as anti-family, anti-religious, foreign, and evil. Over time, Buddhism adopted many Chinese cultural aspects, and monastic lineages that structurally mirrored Confucian family lines appeared, such as in Chan (Zen) Buddhism. There were other ways that Chinese perspectives altered Buddhist traditions: for example, in China eunuchs (who were categorized as queer and excluded in India) were permitted to ordain. At the same time, Buddhism successfully altered Chinese sexual/social relations, adding the category of celibate renunciant to the spectrum of acceptable modes of being.

From historical accounts and modern ethnography and autobiography, we know that there have been many exceptions to the rules in all Buddhist societies. Same-sex activity has always been fairly common in Buddhist monasteries (as in many single-sex environments around the world) and gay, lesbian, intersex, and other persons labeled as queer did sometimes serve as monastics, whether overtly or in the closet. In certain times and places, same-sex relationships were venerated. During the Muromachi period, legends arose in Japan around the iconic tantric monk Kukai and his supposed lover, a novice monk. Eventually manuals arose instructing monks how to seduce and make love to novices, and storybooks about older male-younger male love (samurai or monks) appeared. Some claimed that love between men was actually the purest type of love—a sentiment that is affirming in one sense, but must be recognized as emerging from the valorization of maleness by a deeply patriarchal culture.

As with the recognition of multiple genders in Buddhism, we should be cautious about painting too rosy a picture of queer acceptance in Buddhist societies. Monk-novice relationships were encouraged by some and highly contested by others, and were themselves fraught with power differentials that made them less than perfect models of consent and respect. But they do point to the wider range of possibilities in some Buddhist cultures compared to their European contemporaries.

In the modern era, Buddhist treatment of LGBTQ+ persons and issues spans the entire spectrum. Individuals can face harassment and discrimination in traditionally Buddhist societies. Meanwhile, Taiwan became the first Asian country to legalize same-sex marriage, in part due to activism by the Buddhist nun Shih Chaohwei. Same-sex marriages are not legally recognized in Japan, but some temples—including Jodo Shinshu ones such as Tsukiji Honganji in Tokyo, Saihoji in Nara, and Shofukuji in Nagasaki—do perform them. Perhaps even more significant, given the major role of Buddhism in Japanese death rituals, is the development of same-sex burials. Numerous Jodo Shinshu temples, and some others as well, now offer this option. The most famous gay monk in Japan is the Pure Land Buddhist, make-up artist, and author Nishimura Kodo, who co-developed a rainbow sticker for temples to place at entrances as a signal that they are LGBTQ+-friendly.

To summarize, ignorance of queer issues and needs is very common in Buddhism, and discrimination can be found in some places, though active persecution is rare. Tolerance is increasing in most societies, though concrete progress is often slow.

Queer Aspects of Shinran's Life

Shinran is such a famous monk in Japan that his story is often taken for granted. Furthermore, some of the innovations that he introduced were later made mainstream in Japanese Buddhism. But as I discussed in the first chapter, he was extremely radical in his own time and place. One way that we often fail to appreciate his revolutionary nature is in the potentially queer implications of his biography.

After he was forcibly defrocked by the government and driven into exile, and in opposition to the standard Buddhist division of society into monastics and householders, Shinran boldly declared that he was "neither monk nor layman (sō ni arazu, zoku ni arazu)." He went further than simply making this proclamation: he married and raised children, and at the same time continued to shave his head, wear robes, chant sutras, and preach the Dharma, all of which were activities reserved for monastics. As a married monk, he did not fit into the two accepted Buddhist social categories. Odd as it may seem to us in our day and age to say this of a man deciding to marry a woman, Shinran thereby queered Buddhism, and was arguably queer by the understandings of his own time and place. To state "I am neither monk nor layman" in his own time and place was to make a public statement of a type of queerness.

But this isn't the only queer aspect of Shinran's story. Shinran began as a celibate monk on Mt. Hiei, but he suffered a crisis of confidence and left the mountain in search of answers. He ended up secluding himself at the Rokkakudo chapel, where a statue of

Prince Shotoku was enshrined. Shotoku was one of the earliest major supporters of Buddhism, and later Japanese Buddhists venerated him as an incarnation of the bodhisattva Kannon. This Kannon, known as Avalokiteshvara in Sanskrit, is a resident of the Pure Land and serves as one of Amida Buddha's two main helpers. Shinran undertook the difficult practice of 100 days of circumambulating the statue of Prince Shotoku while chanting nembutsu. This was supposed to purify one's karma and establish a link with the object of veneration. Above all, Shinran, in the dark night of his doubt and despair, was seeking an answer to his existential conflicts.

Month after month Shinran circled the statue, pausing only rarely to answer the call of nature or rest while leaning against the wall. Finally, as he walked toward the end of his retreat, on the ninety-fifth day of practice Shotoku appeared to him in the form of Kannon. The bodhisattva declared that since it was Shinran's karma to violate the precepts, he would become Shinran's wife, have sex with him, act as his life partner, and lead him to the Pure Land. Shinran then left Rokkakudo and joined Honen's emergent Pure Land community. Either at some point while he was studying with Honen or a bit later when he was exiled, Shinran married Eshinni, whom he considered to be an incarnation of Shotoku. In other words, Shinran's wife was a transformed man from a former life, the honored prince, Shotoku.

Shotoku is very much a gender-bending figure in Shinran's thought. In his hymns Shinran ascribed both masculine and feminine qualities to Shotoku, describing the prince at times as a father, at times as a mother:

Great Bodhisattva Avalokitesvara, the world-savior,
Who appeared as Prince Shotoku,
Is like a father, never leaving us,
And like a mother, always watching over us.

From the beginningless past down to the present,
Prince Shotoku has compassionately
Watched over us, like a father,
And stayed close to us, like a mother.

Prince Shotoku, the world savior of great love,
Stays close to us, like a father;
Avalokitesvara, the world savior of great compassion,
Stays close to us, like a mother.

Actually, Shinran was even more explicit than this. We might say that in those three hymns, Shotoku isn't being ascribed with genuine female gender: he's just being said to be intimately close to us, like a mother with her child. But Shinran was also just plain straightforward:

In India, Prince Shotoku
Was born as Queen Srimala,
And in China appeared
As Master Hui-ssu.

He appeared in China
To benefit sentient beings;
He was reborn five hundred times
As both man and woman.

In other words, Shotoku has no essential gender: as a bodhisattva, he transcends gender by being whatever gender the situation requires. This demonstrates Shinran's understanding that gender is not a permanent aspect of the self: it is temporary, fluid, and situational. At the same time, the historical Shotoku was certainly a man, and it was this Shotoku who appeared (as a bodhisattva, to be sure) before Shinran at Rokkakudo and promised to become his wife (that is to say, the woman Eshinni). This doesn't necessarily mean that Shinran experienced same-sex desire in the way we conceptualize such things today. But it certainly means that Shinran, a monk married to a prince in the form of a woman, approached the border of queerness.

Gender is Water, Not Ice

Although Shinran, as usual, took things further than others, and manifested them through concrete action rather than merely in theory, we should perhaps expect a fair degree of accommodation for gender fluidity in Buddhism. According to basic Buddhist philosophy, beings have no inherent, unchanging identity: all aspects of personhood are empty of self-existence and constantly changing. Gender, race, and other particularities of the current moment are just passing phases, therefore. We are female in one life, male in another, queer (in classic Buddhist terms) in yet another, and so on, *ad infinitum*. Shinran affirms in *Tannisho* that all beings have been our mothers and our fathers. This means that every male has been our female relative; every female has been our male relative; we have of course been transgender, bisexual, nonbinary, and every other human possibility, countless times in the past. And whatever we are now, we are headed toward being something different down the road.

Buddhas, as typified by Shakyamuni, are traditionally presented as male, yet they have physical characteristics that are certainly atypical: they have penises that withdraw into their bodies or are hidden in a sheath, leaving them without prominent external genitalia. Meanwhile Kannon, the most popular bodhisattva of all, appears in many forms, both male and female, in the sutras, stories, and art of Asia. Avalokiteshvara was mainly depicted as male in India, but in East Asia transformed to be primarily imagined as a white-cowled woman. In the *Vimalakirti Sutra* an awakened goddess turns into a man while simultaneously transforming the Buddha's chief disciple Shariputra into a woman; the *Lotus Sutra* has a somewhat similar vignette, when an awakened dragon-girl transforms into a man. Other examples abound in Buddhist literature.

In the *Larger Pure Land Sutra*, Amida Buddha's thirty-fifth vow states that women who wish to give up their female gender will not be reborn as women in the Pure Land. This can seem sexist to us today, but my understanding is that it is best seen as pushback against the misogynistic environment of ancient Buddhism. As Buddhism aged, newer generations of monks put ever more stumbling blocks in the path of women. It was said that women were technically capable of awakening but in actuality very inferior at reaching realization of that potentiality; then it was said that

Buddhahood was impossible while still a woman—one would have to undergo at least one more lifetime, as a man, before completing the path; finally, it became common wisdom that women mostly went to the hell realms or took rebirth as hungry ghosts after death.

The *Larger Pure Land Sutra* resists this dire gender-based closure of women's spiritual possibilities: it forthrightly declares that they needn't have any fear, as Amida Buddha will ensure their female state doesn't hold them back. This was a liberating message of comfort in its own time and situation. Shinran certainly understood it in that way. He put it thus in a hymn:

Of the 48 Great Vows,
The 35th in particular
Promises that Amida especially
Extends saving hands to women.

Where previous generations of Buddhists put ever more restrictions and qualifications on women's awakening, Shinran cut through those obstructions to get to the essential point: Amida specifically vowed to liberate women and enable their buddhahood. In fact, women receive special attention in Amida's vows that men do not receive. That is because society stands in the way and hampers women's journey to awakening. Great Compassion sees this unjust barrier and vows to remove it.

Shinran discussed this in another hymn:

Women, the disabled, and those of the two vehicles
Are never born in the Pure Land of happiness as they are;
The sages of the Tathagata's pure lotus
Are born transformed from Dharmakara's lotus of perfect enlightenment.

Here Shinran assures us that—rather than what his society usually taught—women, people with disabilities, and Buddhists of other paths are born as sages in the Pure Land. That they are destined for the same awakened Buddhahood as men, the able-bodied, and so on is the point of his teaching.

This hymn can be misused if we focus on women and others as being lesser-than, which is in no way Shinran's point. That interpretation would suggest that they will be transformed from their femininity, disability, and so on, and become male, able-bodied/minded, etc. This may carry an erroneous sense that there is something wrong with them that must be changed. But they are good and valued just as they are. To understand, we must look to Shinran's next hymn after that one:

> Although there are initially nine grades among practitioners,
> Now [in the Pure Land] there are no distinctions whatever;
> For all are the same in saying the nembutsu,
> following no other way.
> It is like the rivers Tzu and Sheng becoming one taste
> on entering the sea.

As we see, differences in value (the nine grades, which are levels of attainment that were correlated to oppressive class distinctions) are imposed by unenlightened society: they exist *initially*, which is to say, they are believed in by the unawakened discriminatory consciousness. As Shinran indicates, from the perspective of awakened beings of the Pure Land, there are no such distinctions. All are the same as nembutsu practitioners, and all are of the same taste (i.e., emptiness and enlightenment). There is nothing wrong with female bodies or bodies or minds with disabilities, and there is no need to transform them. The need is to transform our vision. Male bodies are not superior, and female bodies are not inferior. Able bodies and neurotypical minds are not superior, and bodies with disabilities or neurodiverse minds are not inferior. Ultimately, even Buddhists of the nembutsu are not superior, and others are not inferior—they're just at different places on the path toward the Pure Land. Amida embraces all.

There are, of course, people who do feel out of place within their bodies. When this is a felt internal mismatch, rather than a socially imposed mandate, transformation may be warranted. The question is always about suffering and its prevention. When ideas about bodily transformation are based on discrimination, they contribute to suffering and should be resisted. Where bodily transformation relieves suffering, it should be supported. In regard to transgender people, the Jodo Shinshu Buddhist Churches of America supports them and the steps necessary for individuals to flourish. In the 1990s, members of the Kangaku, the highest body of doctrinal authorities in Japan, were queried about the appropriateness of conducting a same-sex marriage where one of the partners was transgender. They replied that the ceremony was perfectly fine and appropriate, a tacit admission of support for transgender inclusion in Jodo Shinshu. Now there are ordained transgender and other queer ministers in the BCA.

Compassion in Action

Given that Amida Buddha doesn't discriminate against anyone, and sex and gender are temporary, changing aspects of each person, we might expect Jodo Shinshu to have a good record on gender issues (including acceptance of LGBTQ+ people). The record is *relatively* good, which is not the same as being acceptable. Buddhists always live within the thick weave of culture, and the relatively better support that women have sometimes experienced from major Shin leaders like Shinran and Rennyo must be tempered with recognition that Jodo Shinshu—like other Buddhisms—has often participated in the oppressive patriarchal and heterosexist patterns of Japan (and other countries that it has been carried to). Much work remains to bring daily lifeways and attitudes in harmony with underlying ideals and concepts.

That said, there is significant progress that is worth highlighting. In terms of LGBTQ+ issues specifically, ministers in the Buddhist Churches of America—the largest North American Jodo Shinshu organization—began conducting same-sex marriage ceremonies in the early 1970s, well before any other Buddhists and approximately 40 years before they were legalized at the federal level. In the 1980s the BCA donated money to help establish the first Buddhist AIDS hospice, in San Francisco, and in the 1990s PFLAG (Parents and Friends of Lesbians And Gays) groups began to appear at local Jodo Shinshu temples.

But during this era LGBTQ+ concerns weren't a common topic of public conversation. Rather, ministers cared for individual queer folks on a person-to-person level. Rev. Tesshi Aoyama, who in 1971 became the world's first Clinical Pastoral Education-trained Buddhist hospital chaplain, related just such a fairly standard encounter. A man came to see him at the hospital after reading about Rev. Aoyama in the newspaper. At first, he blustered about the deficiencies of Buddhism, but Rev. Aoyama detected that there was something more at work and asked him to speak his deeper thoughts freely. The man became withdrawn and anxious, unable to find the words he wanted to say. Rev. Aoyama said, "You seem to be suffering a great deal," and the man agreed. Soon he was crying. Finally he worked up his courage and blurted out "I'm gay!"

"I see," Rev. Aoyama replied, and waited to see what the man would say next. The man seemed to be waiting for him to say something, so Rev. Aoyama just said "Yes, I heard what you said," and leaned in a bit to indicate that he was interested in whatever else the visitor had to say. At this the man exclaimed, "Reverend, you surprise me." When he'd confessed his sexuality to Christian ministers in the past, they'd gotten angry and rebuked him, ordering him to repent. "You're not being judgmental about me, are you?" he almost pleaded. Rev. Aoyama assured him he was not. Immediately the man perked back up, regaining the confidence he'd walked in with. He declared this was the first time anyone had tried to understand how he felt as a gay man. He gave his thanks and left. It'd been a hard week at the hospital for Rev. Aoyama, and the conversation had lasted ninety minutes. But he walked out whistling. As he put it: "To think that even I, Tesshi Aoyama, could be of help to someone. My heart was full of satisfaction. I'm sure Shinran Shonin would say, 'How can I judge you? I am, after all, just an ordinary person with all the agonies of lust and desire that you have.'"

After the turn of the millennium, Jodo Shinshu efforts began to swing away from individual support toward active education campaigns, attempts to dismantle heterosexist prejudices and structures within temples, and activism. In 2001 the Hawai'i State Federation of Honpa Hongwanji Lay Associations (a Jodo Shinshu organization) passed a resolution opposing the Boy Scouts of

America's policy against gay scoutmasters. Provoked by President George Bush's use of anti-same-sex marriage rhetoric as a wedge issue in the national election, the BCA Ministers Association passed a resolution in 2004. As the ministers declared:

> Whereas, there is no negative judgment of homosexuality in the Buddhist religion;
> Whereas, a number of BCA ministers have been performing same-sex weddings for a period of at least thirty years;
> Whereas, we wish to affirm the worthiness of all persons independent of sexual orientation;
> Now therefore be it resolved, that the Ministers Association of the Buddhist Churches of America oppose any governmental prohibition of same-sex marriage.

The BCA followed up on this in September 2007 by signing an interfaith "friend of the court" brief to the California Supreme Court declaring that same-sex marriage is a civil right, and its denial violates religious freedom; the Hawaiian Jodo Shinshu temples released their own supportive statement in 2010. In 2013 the BCA Ministers Association went on the record again with a resolution urging the Boy Scouts of America to drop all discrimination against gay scouts and scoutmasters. It was also at this time that BCA temples began participating in annual Pride marches in support of the LGBTQ+ community. Canadian temples as well were publicly voicing their support for queer people and families and participating in Pride events.

Occasional workshops on LGBTQ+ issues had been held by Jodo Shinshu Buddhist organizations since the mid-1990s, but a turning point was reached in 2011, when Rev. Kiyonobu Kuwahara of the Center for Buddhist Education published a searching article asking whether his sangha (and by extension, any Shin temple) was inclusive. The BCA began holding seminars dedicated to education and support around LGBTQ+ issues, starting in 2013 with "Over the Rainbow: The LGBT Community and Shin Buddhism," at the Jodo Shinshu Center in Berkeley. This became an annual event (held in various locations), and was joined by similar seminars and workshops held at local temples. Jodo Shinshu temples created subgroups for support, such as the Lesbian, Gay, Bisexual, Transgender, Queer and Questioning Group at the Buddhist Church of San Francisco and Ichi-Mi at Gardena Buddhist Church. By 2021 at least half of the rising class of Americans training for *kyoshi*, the Dharma teacher certification level that permits a Jodo Shinshu minister to run their own temple, were openly LGBTQ+ (there had already been queer ministers serving BCA temples, but not in large numbers).

It is appropriate to ask why Jodo Shinshu in North America and Hawai'i never expressed condemnation of LGTBQ+ people, and has emerged in recent decades as one of the leaders in queer Buddhist inclusion and support. One key factor is the racial and religious prejudice that Japanese American and Canadian Buddhists experienced since their arrival in the 19th century. Laws prevented them from owning land, voting, and eventually choked off Japanese immigration. Individuals, businesses, and temples faced intimidation, harassment, and violence, culminating in the incarceration of nearly the entire mainland Japanese American and Japanese Canadian population, as well as select members of the Hawaiian population (especially Buddhist ministers) during WWII. The concentration camps were a profoundly traumatic experience, and the sudden and long-term removal caused economic dislocation which cost many families nearly all their possessions (many temples, meanwhile, were vandalized, burglarized, or burnt down).

This history of oppression implanted a deep disgust for all forms of intolerance in the BCA and its sister organizations. Referencing their own history of oppression, Jodo Shinshu Buddhists in Canada and the United States have advocated for the rights of Black people, Muslims, Indigenous people, and other groups, both in their denominational publications and through lobbying the government. When gay and lesbian rights became a major public issue, Shin Buddhists once again looked to their own history for guidance. Articles by, and interviews with, Jodo Shinshu ministers who support same-sex marriage frequently cite the internment experience and extrapolate from the suffering of the Japanese

Americans and Canadians to reject any form of discrimination. For example, Rev. John Iwohara, minister of the Venice Hongwanji Temple, wrote in his temple's newsletter:

> Recently, the issue of equal rights for people who are Lesbian, Gay, Bi-sexual, and Trans-gender (LGBT) has come up again because of the issues surrounding same sex marriage rights. This is an issue that should not simply be ignored. Perhaps Martin Luther King, Jr. expressed it most eloquently when he stated, "Injustice anywhere is a threat to justice everywhere." Because of this, although at first it may not appear that prejudice against the LGBT is my issue, as a Japanese-American man—as a person who had to experience discrimination himself—and a person who has both friends and family who are gay, for me to blindly turn away would be to support and maintain the fact that when the shoe is on the other foot, it kicks just as hard. I want to try to break free from this cycle of abuse.

Ministers in Hawai'i likewise drew on the history of oppression, as in this excerpt from an article on same-sex unions by Rev. Bruce Nakamura:

> While certain leaderships in Hawaii were singled out for the internment camps to the mainland interior, literally all mainland Japanese immigrants living and born during WWII were forcibly relocated. This internment marks a very dark chapter in our national and constitutional history. Out of that period of racial, social, and political injustice, the integrity of the American judicial system was later tested as Japanese Americans demanded remuneration and our government's official apology for having committed a grave betrayal against its own citizens. The shared experiences of the Japanese Americans subject to the war

> years and its aftermath on all fronts deserved not only an honest retelling; it demanded a reclaiming of human truth and justice to safeguard equal protection under the law, not just for most Americans but for all Americans. This tragic drama taught our communities and our nation that no person or group can or should abridge, deny or circumvent the broader right, privilege, and responsibility for equal protection under the law of any person or group based upon race, creed, religion or gender.

There are also specific elements of Shin Buddhism that must be attended to in order to explain the easy acceptance of LGBTQ+ people that most characterizes temples today. In explaining their justification for queer support, North American and Hawaiian Shin Buddhists consistently raise the point that Buddhism has no rules against same-sex partnerships, and that Jodo Shinshu in particular is the least moralistic form of Buddhism. Here for example is the explanation of Rev. Hiroshi Abiko:

> We're short on set rules of conduct. We don't use them as a requirement for being a Jodo Shinshu Buddhist. We don't require people to meditate. We have an openness. The criteria for being a Jodo Shinshu Buddhist is so wide: you just have to be a living being. Of course, as you encounter the teachings, you may begin to reflect on yourself, and begin to investigate the teachings of our founder Shinran. And that may take you all the way back to the words of the Buddha, Siddhartha Gautama. Through this process you come to appreciate all that you have received. Jodo Shinshu is not about following any rules or doing any required practice. It's about getting the meaning of life for yourself and appreciating this life that you are living. In that way, it doesn't matter if you are heterosexual or homosexual, does it? Everyone has a precious life.

Rev. Jerry Hirano of the Salt Lake Buddhist Temple expressed himself thusly:

> In Buddhism, there is no basic difference between homosexuality and heterosexuality.... There have been countless studies showing that homosexuality is natural for the homosexual individual. Homosexuality is a natural response for some human beings and animals, just as heterosexuality is for others. If we agree that sexuality is a natural part of the human psyche, we must ask what is natural about celibacy, which is encouraged by the Catholic priesthood? ... If we were to use the Buddha's words from the Dhammapada to judge homosexuality or in this instance homosexual marriage: "The deed which causes remorse afterwards and results in weeping and tears is ill-done. The deed which causes no remorse afterwards and results in joy and happiness is well done." What do you believe to be the result? I have only observed tears of joy from those couples that were finally recognized as a couple. Why would you deny them that because of your own personal prejudice or discrimination? ... For myself, I have found that I have broken each of these five precepts many times. I try not to break them, but I am weak. As Shinran says, "Immeasurable is the light of Wisdom. Of all beings with limited attributes, none is there unblessed by the Light. Take refuge in true illumination." With my limited attributes I can only try to be mindful of my actions and to try to act without causing harm to others and myself. I really don't have time to be judging others, while trying to be mindful of my own actions. I am grateful that Amida Buddha accepts me as I am. This doesn't mean that I can or will do that for myself or others, only that I will try. As a result, all I can do is to deeply respond with a grateful Namo Amida Butsu.

This discussion can be usefully analyzed because it adeptly lays out the basic North American and Hawaiian Jodo Shinshu approach to ethics, demonstrating a pattern that can be seen in Shin discussions of same-sex relationships, as well as many other issues. Rev. Hirano begins by denying that Buddhism has any strong moral position concerning same-sex attraction or relationships, establishing thereby that the tradition is not homophobic and that Buddhist precepts are not explicit universal commandments to be obeyed. He then lays out an implicit ethical approach to his subject. First, he points out that same-sex attraction is normal for some, and that sexuality in general is natural and healthy (a stance that celibate monastic traditions would not affirm, but which is uncontroversial for the married clergy of Jodo Shinshu). Next, he draws on Buddhist scripture to suggest a situational ethics: that which brings good results is good, rather than rigidly defined set codes of conduct. He then asserts an implied set of moral guidelines: it is the person who seeks to discriminate, rather than the gay person, who is the wrongdoer.

In a distinctive Jodo Shinshu move, however, he then immediately turns the finger of accusation to point at himself. Following Shin Buddhist theory, which asserts that human beings are incapable of fully good behaviour due to our deep self-attachments and therefore must rely on the power of Amida Buddha, Rev. Hirano admits to his own inability to follow the various precepts and places himself on the same level as both the queer person breaking social mores and the bigot violating Buddhist tolerance. From this humbled viewpoint, he asserts that just as he is, he is saved by the Light of Wisdom (i.e., Amida) precisely because Amida Buddha reaches out to all weak and limited beings. He communicates his moral message to potential homophobes that judgmentalism is wrong, but does so not by directly critiquing them, but by rhetorically incriminating himself and thus providing them with a model of proper Shin Buddhist humility in relations with others. In fact, he says that he too may not be able to live without judging, but he will try, and will be accepted either way.

Thus, without ever overtly blaming homophobes, in a few short lines Rev. Hirano flips the issue so that the real moral violation is intolerance rather than same-sex desire, and then pastorally assures those guilty of such ethical lapses that he too is imperfect; furthermore, since his imperfect self is accepted by Amida, there is still a place for them as well. Meanwhile, this change of focus means that queer people are already automatically included. He concludes by suggesting that self-reflection on his own evils leads to grateful awareness of Amida's benevolence (again, serving as a model for the reader to emulate) and that the proper response is saying Namo Amida Butsu.

Analyzed in this way, we can note that Jodo Shinshu is indeed devoid of firm rules, which therefore means that it is open to the possibility of acceptance toward queerness. And despite lacking firm overt rules, it nonetheless affirms an underlying ethical stance, one that values reasoned investigation of each potentially unethical act, holds concern for whether harm is done, and elevates tolerance, humility, and gratitude as moral guides for Buddhist life. This lack of explicit ethical rigidity and appreciation for tolerance naturally made acceptance of same-sex relationships relatively easy once it had risen to a sufficient level of awareness in Jodo Shinshu circles.

A key Buddhist teaching is the doctrine of interconnectedness. Particularly in the Mahayana stream of Buddhism, which includes Pure Land forms such as Jodo Shinshu, Buddhism stresses that all beings and all things in the universe are interrelated with one another. This tends to create a sense of mutuality between self and other, and in the Shin tradition specifically is used to nurture humility in the face of how all other people, animals, plants, and elements work together to contribute to one's life and liberation.

Interconnectedness is raised often in American and Canadian Shin discussions of queer issues. Explaining why he performed same-sex marriages in the 1980s, Dr. Taitetsu Unno said his motivation was "based upon my understanding of the Buddhist teaching of interconnectedness, brought about by deep karmic conditions beyond rational comprehension, which should be cherished, celebrated, and strengthened with the passage of time." In a similar vein, Rev. William Briones wrote on the subject:

> In the *Tannisho* it is written that Shinran said, "All beings have been fathers and mothers, brothers and sisters, in the timeless process of birth and death. When I attain Buddhahood in the next birth, each and every one will be saved." In other words, we are all karmic bound, our lives are interconnected. All beings are equally embraced by Amida Buddha...everyone is included...everyone. As a Jodo Shinshu Buddhist, our goal is to awaken to this spiritual truth of interdependency and equality.

Note how inter-connection is depicted here as inter-dependency, and is evoked in emotional descriptions that depict all beings as kin in a single great family. The concept of interconnection is widely shared among Buddhist groups, since rather than as the product of a creator God, Buddhists believe that all things continually come into existence simultaneously through their mutual interaction. However, we should observe that while it can sometimes have an intellectual or analytical tone when discussed in meditation-based lineages, in Jodo Shinshu interdependence is tied up with emotionally inflected devotional approaches. Thus, interdependence is not simply an idea assented to but is an object of reverence and well of personal meaning, a fundamental orientation for the average Shin Buddhist. Rev. Koshin Ogui put this succinctly: "We focus on life itself. We care about all sentient beings. Buddhism goes beyond human beings; we include cats, dogs, flowers, even mountains and trees. All life. We don't see any [reason for] discrimination."

Most impactful on the Shin discussion of queer inclusion is the core idea of Amida Buddha's all-embracing Primal Vow. Jodo Shinshu is based on the story of Amida Buddha. In the sutras, Dharmakara Bodhisattva (the future Amida Buddha) makes forty-eight vows to create a pure realm of happiness and peace where everyone can swiftly attain buddhahood. The most important of these is the eighteenth vow, wherein Dharmakara vows to save all beings who call on him, without discrimination. This is typically referred to as the Primal or Original Vow of Amida. Jodo Shinshu practice is based on deep trust in the power of Amida's vows, rather than in merit-making, individual meditation practice, or strict personal morality. Shin Buddhist practice therefore takes the form of gratitude for all that one has received in one's life, including the certainty of liberation, instead of striving to achieve buddhahood for oneself. Thus, while Jodo Shinshu is the largest Buddhist tradition in Japan and Hawai'i and one of the most important traditions in North America, it also has some distinctive elements that separate it from other denominations. Dr. Unno asserted that the story of the Primal Vow makes Pure Land Buddhism such as Jodo Shinshu "historically the most inclusive Buddhist salvific scheme."

Virtually all discussions of queer issues in North America and Hawai'i bring up the importance of Amida's Primal Vow. As Rev. Briones states:

> It was out of compassion for all suffering beings that the Bodhisattva Dharmakara established the Forty-eight Vows and became Amida Buddha. Of the Forty-eight Vows, the Eighteenth Vow became the most important to Pure Land Buddhists, since it promised Birth into Amida's Pure Land for those "sentient beings of the ten quarters, with sincere mind entrusting themselves aspiring to be Born in my land and saying my Name perhaps even ten times." However, many of us find it difficult to accept this cosmological story, which took place several kalpas ago. For myself, my understanding of the Dharmakara story is that it represents the deepest aspirations of the human heart that someday all of us will be free of suffering. Amida is a symbol of reality and points to our interdependence to all things and the need to share with others. When the Dharmakara made his Vows, he said: If, when he becomes Buddha, all beings do not experience the same realization, then he would not accept the highest enlightenment. Thus, Dharmakara points out that salvation is not just for himself. Jodo Shinshu, as the way to enlightenment

> must include others, or else there can be no meaning to the Vow. And this I take to heart. Amida's Primal Vow does not discriminate between the young and old, good and evil, ... the rich and poor, Japanese and American, Black and White, gay and straight ... if it doesn't include them ... there can be no meaning to Amida's salvation. It is within Amida's Primal Vow we become aware of the intimate interconnectedness with others. To truly realize this interdependence, one can only manifest a profound sense of responsibility for our fellow human beings.

Another example sheds further light on the issue:

> In the first chapter of the *Tannisho*, Shinran is quoted as saying: "Know that the Primal Vow of Amida makes no distinction between people young and old, good and evil; only shinjin is essential. For it is the Vow to save the person whose karmic evil is deep and grave and whose blind passions abound...." From this, we can see that the compassionate vow of Amida Buddha is intended for all sentient beings. This is the strength of our teaching, but creates a problem for the organization. It is talking about the all-encompassing aspect of the teachings and not necessarily our temples. Most people who talk about the need to open our doors to all people are actually leaving something unsaid. What they are actually saying is, "We need to open our doors to all, like me." People want a temple where there are others with whom they can get along. This is only natural and fine, but it is counter to the spirit of the teachings. Anyone belonging to a group would rather be with people with similar thoughts or at least people they can respect. However, when we think about the spirit of Amida's vow, we can see that it reaches out farther than most of us think or would normally like. Taking the spirit

> of this accepting teaching, we will be accepting of gay marriage and any and all lifestyles, but at the same time, we need to be accepting of all of those who are strongly against these as well. In today's world we would have to expand upon the examples that Shinran gives and include, gay and straight, liberal and conservative, warmongers and peace freaks, pro-life and pro-choice, and so on. We need to be accepting of bigots, racists, terrorists, and any other thing that we may personally despise, but exists.

In this excerpt Rev. Ken Fujimoto tries to speak pastorally to queer people, homophobes, and those caught in the middle. The teaching that Amida accepts everyone means that queer people must be welcomed into the community. But the same teaching also means that homophobes cannot be cast out of the community: Shin Buddhists view them as imperfect beings—like everyone else, themselves included—who need to be cared for, taught a more Buddhist way of being, and affirmed in the universal human family. As someone who wants our temples to be safe places for those who experience marginalization or oppression in general society, this can be a challenge. But so long as people don't act on their prejudices and thereby prevent others from being included, we must continue to embrace those who haven't yet had their hearts opened.

The concept of Amida's Primal Vow accepting every person is the most important key to both why the BCA so easily adopted the performance of same-sex marriages and why the denomination was not torn by major turmoil over LGBTQ+ issues as so many other American religious groups have been. It would be foolish to imagine that Shin Buddhists lack prejudices, always live up to our ideals, or produce perfectly harmonious temple communities devoid of strife or personal animosities. But there is nonetheless a basic and pervasive theological understanding that no one has a firm basis upon which to self-righteously attack anyone else. Therefore, there is little foundation for affirming the exclusion of socially oppressed groups, and a felt need for activists to be understanding of their fellow nembutsu practitioners who are not yet as accepting as they should be.

The Queer Heart of Jodo Shinshu Buddhism

Among the most famous words attributed to Shinran is the simple line: "Even a good person attains birth in the Pure Land, so it goes without saying that an evil person will." This is Shinran's most important teaching in *Tannisho*, and it once again demonstrates his radicalness.

Buddhists of the past and of Shinran's own time all taught that *even an evil person* attains birth in the Pure Land through Amida Buddha's power, so of course that automatically means that *good* people go to the Pure Land. In other words, people were told they had to obey the authorities, and follow the rules, and be good, and they were reassured that because they did so, they were certain to be reborn through the Pure Land: after all, even evil people get to go there, at least theoretically. So, people who were donating to temples and meditating and following the precepts without rocking the boat were put at the centre and told they were the right Buddhists, and those who couldn't do these things were put at the margins and told that although they were inferior, Amida Buddha would eventually save them too.

Shinran absolutely rejected this logic. In fact, he turned it on its head and taught the exact opposite, to reveal the true extent of Amida Buddha's love and compassion. Shinran taught that *even a good person* receives rebirth through the Pure Land way, so therefore it goes without saying that *of course evil people* do so.

Jodo Shinshu spirituality emphasizes that all of us are foolish, ordinary beings who fall far short of buddhahood. We are encouraged to plumb our weaknesses and failings and become aware of our limitations. This leads to a sense of our "evilness," in the way we are stuck in cycles of unwise thought and behaviour, no matter how pious or relatively good we may seem to be. This is part of a simultaneous discovery on the Buddhist path: yes, we are "evil," and yes, we are embraced and affirmed just as we are by Great Compassion.

However, Jodo Shinshu teachings have implications and applications that go beyond the personal spiritual realm. We should note that "evil" is not just a quality that we may discover within our imperfect selves: it is society's term for the unwanted and marginalized. Society decides who it values and who it doesn't value, and then it applies the label of "evil" to those it wishes to oppress, exploit, or exclude. For example, historically-speaking, in Canada and the United States, LGBTQ+ people have been called evil and experienced great suffering due to society's unfair persecution.

Considering Shinran's famous proclamation, we can become aware that Great Compassion embraces *everyone*, including straight people, but only does so *after* embracing queer people first and affirming their inclusion in the sangha of the Pure Land. Shinran understood that Amida Buddha, the Great Compassion, exists to liberate all beings from our suffering. Amida cares about suffering, not about good and evil according to society's definitions. Those who are labeled evil are typically the ones who suffer the most and are given the least optimal circumstances in which to pull themselves up by their bootstraps into nirvana through their own efforts. It is those who need the most help and relief whom Amida liberates *first*—that is to say, those who suffer the most. Therefore, we can rephrase Shinran's teaching as follows: *Even straight people* are liberated by the embrace of the Buddha, so of course LGBTQ+ people are.

With this clarified, we can apply this viewpoint of Great Compassion to our temples. When we do so, we discover that rather than being at the margins of Buddhist life and then grudgingly given a little space within fundamentally straight Buddhist institutions, LGBTQ+ people and queer experiences should actually be recognized as at the heart of Amida Buddha's mission, as being especially the sort of people that Amida seeks to embrace and liberate. LGBTQ+ people—along with women, Black and Indigenous people, and others who have been labeled evil—are not an after-thought for the Buddha: they are a first priority. We too should prioritize listening to their experiences, sharing in the Dharma with them, and expressing gratitude that everyone, queer and straight, is included in the Buddha's Vow.

3

Refugee Shinran

In the first chapter, I described Shinran as a radical—indeed, perhaps the most radical Buddhist that Japan has ever produced. Naturally the question arises: where did this radicalness come from? Was it simply part of Shinran's unusual character? Was he raised to be a rebel? Or did something in his life awaken him to such an extent that he took the Buddhist tradition further than anyone before him?

It's impossible to fully know another person and their motivations, especially someone of a different culture far away in time and place. And yet, there are some clear clues that indicate at least part of how Shinran came to be such a radical Buddhist. The personal hardships that Shinran faced profoundly influenced the Buddhism that he taught. This is true of his descendent Rennyo as well. The ways in which these men responded to the troubles of their times with Buddhist messages designed to provide insight, comfort, and solidarity to their listeners show that Buddhism is not static or timeless. Rather, Buddhism emerges from the social conditions and life experiences of those who practice and teach it.

In this chapter, I want to explore how the persecution, displacement, and poverty that Shinran and Rennyo experienced led them to feel solidarity with the neglected, the abused, the shunned, and the refugee. Their responses took two main forms: first, they placed themselves among such marginalized people, rather than apart from them. Second, they promoted a vision of Buddhism that focused on images of peace, shelter, security, welcoming, and universal compassion. It was these two aspects—identity with the outcastes of society, and the propagation of Buddhism that accepts and cares for all—that fundamentally defined

Jodo Shinshu as a radical teaching for people living in hard times.

Shinran Shonin: Downwardly Mobile

The person who we refer to as Shinran was born in 1173 CE, in a hamlet on the outskirts of the capital, Kyoto. Many of the details of his life are uncertain, and there are debates within the scholarly community over various elements of his autobiography. His childhood name was Matsuwakamaro. His family seems to have been part of the lower aristocracy, so while they were not people of significant power or importance, his initial childhood would have been relatively comfortable. Unfortunately for him, it was all downhill from there.

His father apparently died when Shinran was around four years old, and Shinran became an orphan at age nine. We don't know the precise causes of his parents' death, but it occurred in the midst of the Genpei War, a civil war that brought about the destruction of the emperor-based form of government and the ascendency of the warrior class as a military dictatorship that ruled Japan for nearly 700 years. There could be any number of reasons why Matsuwakamaro was orphaned, as it was an age of numerous disasters. The horror of the times was described by the Buddhist hermit monk Chomei in his *Account of a Ten Foot Hut*:

> In the reign of Emperor Yowa [1181], I believe, though it becomes so long ago I have trouble remembering, there was a terrible famine, lasting for two years [this is the period when Shinran became an orphan]. From spring through summer there was a drought, and in autumn and winter typhoon and flood—bad conditions one after another, so that grain crops failed completely. Everything people did became wasted effort. Though they prepared the ground in the spring, and transplanted the rice in the summer, the fall's rice harvest and winter's prosperity were not achieved.... After a year of such suffering, people hoped the new year would be better, but the misery increased as, in

> addition to the famine, people were afflicted by contagious disease. Everyone suffered from malnutrition, until gradually to say that "All the fish will choke in shallow water" would fit very well. Now even those wearing bamboo hats, with legs wrapped in leggings, walked frantically from house to house begging. I saw vagabonds of this kind, as they were walking, suddenly collapse and die. Close to the roofed mud wall at the side of the road, the number of bodies dead from starvation continually increased. Because no one even tried to clear away those corpses, the odor of the putrefaction became offensive throughout [Kyoto], and people could not even stand to look at them. The city was permeated by the smell, and the mountain of corpses accumulated along the Kamo riverbed until there were places where horses and carriages could not pass.

Amidst all this death, Matsuwakamaro was taken to the Shorenin temple in Kyoto. Parentless children had few options in medieval Japan, and the monastery was the only place to receive social services. The pathos of life seems to have already imprinted itself upon the boy. Tradition records that when the abbot Jien suggested a slight delay in his ordination, the future Shinran replied with a poem: "The minds that think there is a tomorrow are like cherry blossoms; but who can tell if there will be a tempest in the night?" He was ordained right away, and became Hannen, a novice monk. Thus, he passed out of the world of family and prestige to become a servant of the temple.

Hannen went to work at Enryakuji, the Tendai Buddhist complex on Mt. Hiei, at the northeastern edge of Kyoto. He laboured and trained there, taking a position as a fellow in the hall dedicated to Pure Land practice. But after twenty years of effort, he concluded that he had reached a dead-end. Tendai was the most powerful sect of Buddhism in Japan, with royal patronage, massive temples, and an elaborate curriculum designed to transform practitioners into awakened bodhisattvas who mastered the entirety of Buddhism on behalf of other beings. Yet when he looked around himself at the place he'd called home for two decades, he saw corruption and decadence, with a noticeable lack of enlightened success stories among his peers. As he described it later, "As a mark of increase in the five defilements, all monks and laypeople of this age behave outwardly like followers of the Buddhist teaching, but in their inner thoughts, believe in nonbuddhist paths.... Each of us, in outward bearing, makes a show of being wise, good, and dedicated; but so great are our greed, anger, perversity, and deceit, that we are filled with all forms of malice and cunning." Much worse, when he looked inside himself he found that his years of Buddhist practice had not created a transformation in his own character: "This self is false and insincere; I completely lack a pure mind.... Extremely difficult is it to put an end to our evil nature; the mind is like a venomous snake or scorpion. Our performance of good acts is also poisoned; hence, it is called false and empty practice.... I am without shame and self-reproach, and lack a mind of truth and sincerity.... Lacking even small love and small compassion, I cannot hope to benefit sentient beings."

Ruthless in his self-examination, Shinran realized that the Tendai way was inadequate to bring someone such as himself to Buddhahood. Lamenting, he came down from the mountain, and joined the breakaway community of the monk Honen, in the Yoshimizu area of Kyoto. In the process he once again lost his home and those he cared about, and experienced a further step down the social ladder. He also experienced another change in his identity, as Honen renamed him Shakku.

Honen was a widely respected monk. But his new community was a mixed group of monks, nuns, and laypeople, marginal to established society and in a precarious position in relation to the powerful Buddhist temples. Worse yet, their doctrine and practices represented a profound threat to entrenched Buddhist power structures. Honen was a radical like his disciple Shakku (Shinran): he had thrown out nearly every form of Tendai practice, insisting instead that simply saying the nembutsu was fully sufficient to enter the Pure Land and achieve Buddhahood. This directly undercut the *raison d'être* for the established monasteries and their social privileges, as elite Buddhism taught that it was only through the herculean efforts of the pure monastic practitioners that Buddhahood was possible. These special adepts needed to be respected and deferred to, as their prayers and transference of merit (in exchange for donations) were the only access regular people had to good karma that could stave off poverty, violence, ruin, and rebirth in the suffering hell realms. Women in particular were oppressed by mainstream Buddhism, which preached that their female gender was a karmic punishment due to previous evil, and that their polluting bodies and wicked ways doomed them to unfavourable rebirths. But if Honen and his followers were right, then women and men were capable of the same practices and every peasant and enslaved person could expect the same destination as the aristocrats—and thus there was no need to pay for the elaborate ceremonies and paraphernalia that the Buddhist establishment demanded.

The entire social system of feudal Japan appeared to be in danger, and subjugation was inevitable. Buddhist monks in the elite monasteries trumped up charges against Honen's community, and a scandal occurred when some of Honen's disciples taught the nembutsu to the emperor's concubines and convinced them to commit to Buddhist practice. Swiftly, the nembutsu was outlawed and the community was forcibly disbanded. Four of Honen's disciples were executed, while Shinran, his elderly teacher Honen, and several of his peers were stripped of their ordinations by the government, which had total control over Buddhism. They were branded as felons—Shinran's monastic name was taken away from him and he was forced to use the criminal name Fujii Yoshizane—and driven into exile far from their homes in Kyoto. For seeking a path that was open to all and helping to preach that Buddhism could be for everyone, Shinran found himself a refugee.

Refugee Buddhism

Exile was a bitter punishment for Shinran, but it was also the spark that transformed his Dharma teaching. In the distant countryside, Shinran was forced for the first time to truly live among the common people. What he discovered through his suffering and that of those around him strengthened his commitment to the Pure Land tradition. He refused to stop teaching Buddhism: in fact, his exile gave him the chance to preach to the disenfranchised masses who'd been left out of the establishment way of Buddhism. His disciples included farmers, peasants, townspeople, merchants, low-ranking samurai, and women. Sitting with them, listening to their problems, his understanding of the vastness of Amida Buddha's compassion in the face of the world's overwhelming suffering expanded.

Studying the teachings of Shinran, it's clear that the persecution, displacement, and poverty he experienced led him to feel solidarity with the neglected, the abused, and refugees. Oral testimony records an event where he was invited to a feast, but he didn't sit with the high monks, as was his right. Instead, he went and sat among the commoners and novices, eating with them, and treating them as peers, a major breach of medieval social protocol. His social consciousness had been fundamentally awakened. As he put it in a verse:

The petitions of the wealthy
Are like putting stones into water;
The claims of the poor
Are like putting water into stone.

The Buddhism of Shinran's time was primarily designed for the privileged. Difficult practices of meditation and study for literate elites, merit reaped from large donations of money and land, strict precepts for those who didn't have to get their hands dirty—these were the currency of medieval Japanese Buddhism. But Shinran felt for the poor and downtrodden. After living on the mountaintop, he eked out an existence as an exile and criminal among the common folk. His Buddhism was sighted from the ground floor, where regular people's cries failed to shift the immovable weight of social oppression from higher-positioned elites. Thus, the Buddhism he developed was focused on the needs of the poor and abandoned. Jodo Shinshu from the beginning was a poor man's Buddhism, and it is from this origin that its spiritual and social revolutionary potential sprang.

Shinran's embrace of the marginalized and displaced caused him to focus on images of peace, shelter, security, welcoming, and universal compassion in his teachings. We can see this, for instance, in a passage he provides in *Kyogyoshinsho*, his magnum opus: "The Pure Land is free forever from slander and dislike; all are equal, with no anxieties or afflictions. Whether human or deva, good or evil, all can reach the Pure Land. On attaining it, their distinctions vanish; all equally enter the stage of non-retrogression.... Through the power of the Buddha's Vows, the karmic evil of the five grave offenses and the ten transgressions is eradicated and all are brought to attainment of birth. When those who slander the dharma or abandon the seed of Buddhahood turn about at heart, they all reach the Pure Land." This is a remarkable message, as it teaches that even those who commit the worst crimes and are excluded from the Pure Land according to the doctrines of the other schools, are actually embraced by the Buddha and admitted to the Pure Land along with those of whom society approves.

Shinran often adapted his teachings into forms that his illiterate followers could access. He wrote repetitive letters in ordinary language that could be read aloud to gatherings of labourers, and he crafted a huge volume of songs that expressed the Dharma in concrete images that anyone could memorize and understand. The flavour of his Dharma can be gleaned by examining some of these hymns.

The liberating wheel of light is without bound;
Each person it touches, it is taught,
Is freed from attachments to being and nonbeing,
So take refuge in Amida, the enlightenment of nondiscrimination.

Shinran sings that Amida Buddha is the light of liberation, the light of nondiscrimination. All who encounter this light are moved beyond their painful self-centred attachments. This light enables a healing perspective that cares for all, not just oneself or those like oneself.

The light of purity is without compare.
When a person encounters this light,
All bonds of karma fall away;
So take refuge in Amida, the ultimate shelter.

Amida Buddha is the ultimate shelter for all those without security: refugees; the unhoused; the lost; the dispossessed; the heartbroken. The purpose of Amida is to destroy bondage, enacting liberation.

The cloud of light is unhindered, like open sky;
There is nothing that impedes it.
Every being is nurtured by this light,
So take refuge in Amida, the one beyond conception.

The cloud of light is the compassionate wisdom that reaches all. Nothing can prevent it from embracing everyone. While we provisionally call it Amida, we are speaking about something ultimately beyond conception: the deepest truth of emptiness and the liberated buddha-mind, which is given freely to all.

The light of compassion illumines us from afar;
Those beings it reaches, it is taught,
Attain the joy of dharma,
So take refuge in Amida, the great consolation.

Shinran calls Amida great consolation. The light of compassion shines for those who suffer from oppression, loss, depravation, and endangerment. Ignoring no one, it provides the joy that life in the Dharma brings.

Their countenances, dignified and wonderful,
are beyond compare;
Their bodies, delicate and subtle, are neither human nor deva.
Theirs is the body of emptiness, the body of boundlessness,
So take refuge in Amida, the power of nondiscrimination.

Shinran speaks of the beings reborn through the Pure Land way. As they realize nirvana, they understand the emptiness of themselves and their boundless interrelation with all others. Instead of the conventional view that women and commoners' bodies were defiled, dishonorable, and needed to be restrained, Shinran taught that everybody was destined to become boundless and beyond the control of the authorities.

Beings born in the Pure Land in the past, present, and future
Are not solely from this world;
They come from Buddha lands throughout the ten quarters
And are countless, innumerable, beyond calculation.

Shinran preached that the number of beings reborn through the Pure Land way is countless, infinite. No one in any state of life or any place whatsoever is left out. Instead of the conventional view that few people qualified to be admitted to the Pure Land, Shinran declared that the gates of the Pure Land are wide open, ready for all to be embraced and liberated together as members of Amida Buddha's sangha.

As we can see, Shinran taught his followers that Amida Buddha accepts everyone, leaves no one out, can cross any border, cannot be impeded in the quest to liberate all, is unrestricted, non-discriminating, offering consolation, emancipation, and shelter to all who suffer. This isn't some stock list of qualities: these vibrant images and ideas are drawn from Shinran's own experiences and were meant to offer solace to refugees, prisoners, outcastes, and the downtrodden. Depicting the Buddha as "the ultimate shelter" isn't a teaching aimed at those who've never had to worry about having a roof over their heads.

Rennyo: Monshu on the Run

Shinran's radical teaching spread gradually through Japan until the lifetime of Rennyo, known as the second founder of Shin Buddhism. A direct descendent of Shinran, he was born in the 15th century (about 150 years after Shinran) as the bastard son of the head of one of the main Jodo Shinshu organizations. His mother was a servant who was sent away when he was six years old; he never saw her again, despite years of searching for her. He was persecuted by his stepmother, who wanted her own son to inherit the lineage, and Rennyo grew up in poverty, eating one meal a day, without hot water. He studied Shinran's teachings by moonlight since there was no money for lamp oil.

Due to his natural aptitude, Rennyo eventually did become *monshu* [spiritual leader] of the Honganji tradition, and thus he was the inheritor of Shinran's lineage. But his status as *monshu* didn't lead to an easy life. Unlike the heads of monastic lineages, he couldn't afford servants, so he washed his babies' dirty diapers himself. Rennyo lived through the decade-long Onin War, which kicked off 100 years of civil war in Japan. He was widowed four times and buried seven sons and daughters during his long life. But perhaps most importantly, like Shinran he ended up as a refugee.

Two hundred years after the death of Shinran, his Dharma teaching was still seen as radical and profoundly dangerous, especially to the elite Buddhist institutions. In 1465, warrior monks from the monastery on Mt. Hiei attacked and destroyed the Honganji, Rennyo's temple. Rennyo barely escaped with his life. As he fled, he carried with him the sacred statue of Shinran that has been enshrined at Honganji. Carved in his likeness, the statue's lacquer was mixed with Shinran's ashes, and served as a deeply important memorial to the founder. For years afterwards, Rennyo was forced to flee from place to place, a refugee and migrant, frequently homeless and always in danger. Finally he settled in remote, wild Yoshizaki, far from those who wanted to destroy the Pure Land movement.

Rennyo's poverty and refugee experiences deeply stamped his Dharma teaching. Whereas other leaders of his time taught from high platforms, emphasizing the social and spiritual superiority of high monks, Rennyo sat on the ground with his commoner followers. He personally served them sake and listened to their troubles. Following Shinran's example, he wrote teaching letters in the vernacular, using common idioms of the time that regular people could understand and relate to. He stressed anjin (peaceful heart) in a war-torn time. Through Rennyo's teaching, forged in his experiences of suffering and exile, Jodo Shinshu became the largest school of Buddhism in Japan.

If anything, Rennyo's life of depravation and exile led him to become even more appreciative of what he did have. In accordance with Shinran's understanding that the Jodo Shinshu path is one of thankfulness and grateful nembutsu, he expressed his feelings of gratitude over and over. These are well captured in some of his recorded sayings. "Even when I drink water from the well, it is through the working of true reality. I understand that I owe even a mouthful of water to the working of the Buddha.... When I take meals, I never forget the benevolence of the Buddha. With every mouthful, I am reminded of this benevolence." Even more simply, he stated "I eat and dress myself through the benevolence of the Buddha."

This spirit continues in modern-day Jodo Shinshu. Rev. Ryoko Osa of the West Covina Buddhist Temple put it well when she wrote,

> "People who have not heard of the Buddhist teaching are likely to think that the words 'Namu Amida Butsu' are some kind of mysterious words with magical power. In fact, the words 'Namu Amida Butsu' is a wish that means, 'Let me live my life by entrusting myself to the Immeasurable wisdom and compassion.' This Immeasurable wisdom and compassion are the power that makes us realize that our lives are sustained by all of the other immeasurable elements in this world. We need the sun, water, air, earth, trees to live, do we not? But also we need the people who provide us with drinking water and vegetables and so on. I cannot live alone even for a single moment without these other resources. And this is true for all existence: nothing can exist alone. All things exist thanks to all the other things that support their life. If we realize this truth, we can say that we have received 'the calling of Immeasurable wisdom and compassion' symbolized by Namu Amida Butsu."

Our Refugee Legacy and Responsibility

Shinran and Rennyo experienced exile many centuries ago. But the refugee experience is one that is close to the heart of the Jodo Shinshu experience in North America today. Unfortunately, unjust persecution is hardly a thing of the past.

A few hours after the Japanese surprise attack on Pearl Harbor, the bishop of the Hawaiian Jodo Shinshu temples was arrested and taken to a prison camp. He was the first internee, targeted because the Buddhist temples were seen as the biggest threats to America. Soon, other Buddhist ministers were taken away, with some of them sent to labour camps. Eventually over 140,000 people of Japanese descent were incarcerated in North America, two-thirds of them Americans or Canadians by birth, and most of those children. While Christians were also unjustly incarcerated, the government's action was overtly anti-Buddhist. Buddhist and Shinto leaders in Hawai'i and on the West Coast were the first to be arrested and received the greatest surveillance; the American authorities often favoured Christians over Buddhists, even though Buddhists outnumbered Christians two to one in the camps. Just being Buddhist was a strike against prisoners when they were considered for early release, better camps, or other privileges. Buddhist temples throughout North America and Hawai'i were shuttered, with many seized as barracks or subjected to vandalism or arson. For those who were sent away, they were forced to sell their property, or it was seized and sold by the government, which then used the funds to pay for the imprisoned victims' confinement. Families languished behind barbed wire in searing deserts or freezing mountain valleys, incarcerated simply for who they were. Most of these victims were Jodo Shinshu Buddhists.

After years of confinement in military camps, the War Relocation Authority sought to resettle the prisoners in a dispersal pattern away from the West Coast. The idea was to spread them so thinly throughout the rest of the country that the Japanese would vanish into the greater population and cease to be a cohesive community. It was this policy of official pressure that led to temples in the East, such as in Chicago and Cleveland. The situation was even worse in Canada—Japanese Canadians were barred from returning to the West Coast until 1949, long after the war had ended. Thus, even after incarceration by their own governments, many families emerged from the camps only to become internal refugees. Thousands of people in both countries were deported, including many who'd never lived in Japan. For those who made it back to California, Oregon, and Washington, many returned to nothing. The temples were converted into hostels, where refugees from the camps lived until independent living situations could be found. In some cases, non-Japanese who'd occupied the temples during the war refused to leave and had to be sued to regain possession.

All told, the internment and attacks on Japanese North American communities dealt a profound blow to Buddhism, which was radically reshaped by the experiences of persecution and the trauma of incarceration. Our temples are the survivors of oppression and exile, whose legacy continues more than two generations after the end of the war. The temples became literal places of refuge, the only safe and secure community gathering spots in a racist and intolerant white Christian society.

The experiences of Shinran and Rennyo weren't simply misfortunes that they endured. They were the very soil from which the universal teaching of Jodo Shinshu sprang. To remain faithful to the all-embracing vision that they bequeathed to us, we must carry forward their wisdom. We must never forget the hard lessons about racism, exclusion, and injustice that were learned in the WWII persecution. We need to make sure that our temples are truly welcoming spaces that push back against the exclusion and suspicion that we see all around us in society. To carry forward the Dharma of Shinran and Rennyo, we must take care of those in need, especially refugees and the dispossessed, whether around the world or in our neighborhoods. And most importantly, we have to overcome fear and prejudice by relying on the light of nondiscrimination that embraces and accepts everyone, and promises them shelter. In the next chapter I discuss how we might approach the challenges of suffering caused by dispossession, in relation to the Jodo Shinshu experience.

4

Buddhism in the Age of the Refugee

In the previous chapter, I described how the real-life experiences of exile and persecution led Shinran and Rennyo to understand and teach in ways that were oriented towards suffering people. In this chapter, I discuss some of the current-day challenges that we face and consider how Jodo Shinshu's inherent orientation toward relieving the suffering of those experiencing displacement and oppression may operate in relation to them. This is a way for me to grapple with such issues as homelessness, the refugee crisis, undocumented immigration, mass incarceration, and risks around climate change, which are connected problems revolving around borders, movement, our responsibilities to one another, and the vulnerabilities of those who cannot determine for themselves where or how they will live. No matter our personal political opinions, these are dire challenges that we will need to face together.

Challenges and the state of the world today

According to the United Nations Refugee Agency at the time of this writing, there are nearly 90 million displaced persons in the world. That is more people than you will ever know, meet, or even pass on the street in your entire lifetime. From this number, more than 36 million are officially categorized as refugees, meaning that they have been expelled from their home countries, and are unable to return. For our purposes, I think we should adopt a more expansive understanding; really, a refugee is anyone who has been unwillingly forced from their home, regardless of which side of a political border they currently happen to be on. It is certainly possible to be a refugee within one's own nation. There is deep truth in the observation of the Chilean playwright and human rights activist Ariel Dorfman that "we live in the age of the refugee."

Between 2010 and 2020 the number of refugees in the world doubled, and the rate of displacement continues to accelerate. This global refugee crisis has led to mass migration of displaced people across entire continents, often experiencing exploitation and abuse by the governments and people of the countries they are forced to pass through. There is a common tendency by reactionary governments to paint refugees as a security concern, but more than 40 percent of refugees in the world are children, and the real horrors that refugees are escaping are profoundly worse than the extremely low level of violence committed by refugees admitted into new host countries. When refugees are banned, such as occurred in the United States under Donald Trump, it is mainly suffering children and their families who are excluded.

Naturally, when we think about refugees, we primarily assume them to be victims of war. That's certainly a major part of the picture and will continue to be so. But there are also new causes that are increasing and will ever-more add their own forms of misery to life. One of these is the effects of human-caused climate change, which are not restricted to nations or areas experiencing violence. According to our best current scientific analysis, sea level rise will displace 13 million Americans by the year 2100; by then, South Florida and much of the Gulf Coast will be underwater. Phoenix, currently one of the fastest growing cities in the United States, will be uninhabitable, with summertime temperatures exceeding the highest temperature that has ever been recorded on Earth. Western Canada and the United States will experience thousands of dangerous wildfires every year. Closer in time to our present moment, 1.5 billion people live in regions that will develop desert-like conditions by the year 2050, and approximately a quarter of the world's species will have gone extinct. By the time you've finished reading this chapter, Louisiana will have lost an area the size of a football field due to rising sea level-based erosion.

And that's just the approaching *normal* state of things—to add to that, the recent climate change-related hurricane disasters in New Orleans, Houston, and Puerto Rico, devastating floods in

Afghanistan, Germany, and Nigeria, mudslides in British Columbia, and deadly waves of heat and fire along the West Coast point towards the increasing frequency of dramatic emergencies that will overwhelm our political, technological, and economic resources. As all this rolls on and on, in the future there will be ever more of us, living on ever less land, with ever less of that land being arable, and under constant threat of super storms, wildfires, and other violent weather events. Our grandchildren and their families will live out their entire lives being just one storm away from becoming refugees themselves.

Related to all of this, water conflicts are projected to become one of the hottest flashpoints for international warfare in the future. Mass migrations of people due to war and climate change put increased stress on water systems not designed to accommodate such sudden influxes, and resulting pressures will combine with rising scarcity to create crises around the world, leading to more violence, which will produce more refugees, and so on, in a grim cycle.

Of course, land insecurity and disputes over borders are hardly new issues. Perhaps no communities know this better than Indigenous peoples. Hundreds of unique cultures existed throughout the Americas and Hawai'i prior to colonization, but contact with the people of Europe brought disastrous violence, illness, oppression, and, especially, theft of their lands and resources. Colonization is the most extreme form of land insecurity possible, essentially turning entire nations into visitors, vagrants, or serfs in their own homeland, while replacing them with invaders. It's perhaps only matched by the evils of the trans-Atlantic trade in enslaved African persons, which forcibly relocated approximately 12 million people across the world for their total exploitation. Today the repercussions of colonization, slavery, and ongoing discrimination continue to have deep negative impacts among communities of colour, and remain constant points of friction that tatter North America's social fabric.

One of these repercussions is mass incarceration, which Indigenous and Black communities experience at greatly disproportionate rates, and which has become tied to insidious systems of political and economic profiteering. In Canada, where Indigenous people are five percent of the general population, they make up nearly a third of all federal inmates (and 70 percent of inmates in Manitoba); Indigenous women comprise 50 percent of the female federal prison population, and nearly 100 percent of girls in Saskatchewan youth jails are Indigenous. In the United States, Black people are less than 14 percent of the population but make up more than 38 percent of inmates. Unjust or extreme forcible confinement is as much a human rights issue as forced relocation, and is related to the same problems of insecurity, displacement, and oppression.

Much of the discussion about borders is clearly dominated by fear of foreigners, which is frequently expressed through alarm cries about "illegal immigration." Indeed, politicians regularly use immigration as a wedge issue to get elected, or to distract from other policies which they don't wish to receive scrutiny—and it serves as a dog-whistle for racists and xenophobes who are increasingly emboldened to bring their hates and fears into our public places. Concrete manifestations of these tendencies include Donald Trump's proposed wall along the U.S.-Mexican border and the racist American ban on travel by citizens of several majority Muslim countries from 2017-2021.

Of course, when speaking of unauthorized immigration, we must consider the causes, which include economic and political exploitation of other countries, especially in Latin America, and the motivations for immigration, which are mainly the universal human search for a better life for oneself and one's children. Despite right-wing rhetoric to the contrary, undocumented immigrants are less likely to commit crime than citizens, and the economic contributions they make through taxes, consumption, and labour exceed the costs of the services they receive. Perhaps the most poignant group of all are the so-called Dreamers, the hundreds of thousands of young people raised in the United States as Americans, who face possible deportation to countries that are totally foreign to them.

For the Dreamers, America is the only real home they've ever known. Meanwhile, close to 600,000 Canadians and Americans live amongst us with no home to call their own. Homelessness is on the rise: from Ottawa to Honolulu, local governments have had to declare states of emergency over the homelessness crisis. The causes of homelessness are multiple, but especially relate to failures on the part of society to properly manage situations of which policymakers are already well aware. For example, there are only twelve counties in the entire United States (out of more than 3000) where it would be possible to rent a one-bedroom home, based on the state or federal minimum wage. Gentrification has driven large numbers of families from homes they previously afforded, and destroyed entire long-standing communities, largely benefitting wealthy and enfranchised members of society at the expense of the poor and people of colour. The profoundly unequal distribution of wealth in America, one of the richest societies in the history of our species, means that 71 percent of white-identified Americans own their homes, but only 41 percent of African-Americans can say the same—naturally, this means that they are especially vulnerable to disruptions that can lead to homelessness, on the one hand, or incarceration on the other. The unhoused population of the USA includes approximately 60,000 families with children, and 25 percent of those dealing with homelessness are employed yet cannot afford permanent housing.

Truly, we face unprecedented challenges. Suffering related to displacement is all around us, at our borders, in our streets, and in our own temples, churches, schools, and homes.

Buddhist Refugees

I believe the issues that we face are relevant to all of us, because we share the same world, and no matter where you fall on the political spectrum or what your identity or commitments, we all have the capacity to feel empathy and to be a force for good. I also feel there are particular reasons why Buddhists should pay close attention to the problems of present-day refugees and others struggling with displacement. Buddhists ourselves have often been refugees, especially in recent times. Recalling our community's suffering should motivate us to help with the suffering of those around us, whether or not they happen to be Buddhist as well.

My particular expertise as a scholar is in the history of Buddhism in North America and Hawai'i. This history is often told as a success story: in this story, Buddhism moves from the fringes into a position of relative mainstream acceptance and contribution to the North American tapestry of faith and culture. From the mindfulness movement to the Zen-like wisdom of Jedi master Yoda, there are few North Americans today whose lives haven't been touched in some fashion by Buddhism. It has been observed that the United States is the most diverse Buddhist nation on Earth, since it has all the major forms of world Buddhism coexisting in the same society. By this measure, Los Angeles is among the most important Buddhist cities on the planet, ranking in its own way alongside Lhasa or Kyoto.

If the story of Buddhism in North America is one of success, we should note that it has involved considerable cost along the way. When reflecting on why Los Angeles is so diverse, for example, we must face the fact that this diversity is the direct result of war, suffering, and displacement. The Buddhist Vietnamese American, Cambodian American, and Lao American communities were primarily established by refugees seeking solace from the profound violence unleashed in Southeast Asia by the American war in Vietnam. The context for the war was centuries of Western colonization in Asia, and ongoing 20th century imperialism by both capitalist and Communist factions. Refugee Buddhist communities came here seeking a better life than that provided in the camps, but of course they would have preferred the possibility of returning to their homelands with safety and security. This was true as well for significant numbers of Chinese Americans, Mongolian Americans, and some Sri Lankan Americans, who arrived not as eager immigrants, but as fleeing victims of war and oppression.

Perhaps the most famous case currently is the Tibetan diaspora. Prior to the Communist Chinese takeover of Tibet, and the subsequent exodus of the Dalai Lama and his supporters, there was literally no presence of Tibetan Buddhism in the West, and it was one of the least understood major forms of Buddhism. Today, Tibetan Buddhism is one of the most popular and recognizable forms: books by Tibetan authors appear on the bestsellers lists; half of Hollywood seems to have a guru; and images of Tibetan monks are used to sell everything from computers to sneakers. While we can appreciate the positive contributions that Tibetans have made to North American and world culture, we should not forget that nearly all Tibetans in North America are refugees, sharing their religious resources as much out of the necessity for cultural and economic survival as from any missionary impulse.

If we look back into the North American Buddhist past, we inevitably confront the effects of profound racism and xenophobia. Today, Asian Americans make up less than six percent of the U.S. population, with many of those being relatively recent immigrants. The reason for this low percentage of the population is due solely to racist border laws progressively enacted over nearly a century, beginning in the 1870s. In an effort to protect white power and Christian superiority, the Chinese, Japanese, and eventually all Asians were targeted for immigration bans, violence, and discrimination, both legal and otherwise. The culmination of this trajectory occurred with the WWII incarceration of Japanese Americans and Japanese Canadians, as described in the previous chapter.

Buddhists, both in Asia and North America, have experienced the suffering of violence, systematic expulsion from their homes, and mass displacement. It is important to keep this history of persecution in mind when approaching the present-day issues of refugees, the unhoused, immigrants, and the prison industry. However, it is perhaps even more urgent that we become aware of how Buddhists too have participated in the displacement and genocide of unwanted groups. Buddhists are not only victims, but also victimizers. This is nowhere more horrifically clear than in the ongoing genocide being committed against the Rohingya Muslim community of Myanmar.

Since 2016, the Myanmar military, with aid from paramilitary neighborhood groups, has carried out extreme violence against the Muslim population of the western Rakhine state. A systematic campaign of murder, rape, and arson drove over a million people from their villages in a matter of mere months. Almost the entire Rohingya population now lives in makeshift Bangladeshi camps, including the largest refugee camp in the world: these are places of profound danger and crowding that face peril when the monsoon season arrives. Back in Myanmar, the military has bulldozed their homes, torn down their community centres, and destroyed their fields, until virtually no trace of their presence is left. Return to their villages appears to be impossible; absorption into Bangladesh or other nearby countries is both difficult and unwanted by those nations; but continuance in the camps is a sentence for death for many, and misery for all.

And amidst the almost unfathomable suffering of the Rohingya, one of the most disturbing facts is that this genocide was cultivated and carried out by Buddhists and in the name of Buddhism, and that among the most extreme firebrands in the anti-Rohingya movement are *ordained Buddhist monks*. Their leader is Ashin Wirathu, a man so violent in his rhetoric that he has been called the Buddhist Bin Laden. Prior to the August attacks, he spent years stoking the fires of hatred toward Muslims in Myanmar, preaching that they were subhuman: Rohingya, he alleged, were reincarnated dogs and vermin who represented a dire threat to Burmese society and moral values. He spun elaborate conspiracy theories about how the Rohingya, less than two percent of Burmese society prior to their expulsion, sought to take over the country from within and convert it to Islam. Wirathu supported policies that made it illegal for Muslims to marry Buddhists, that deprived them of their freedom of movement within the country, and that refused to grant them citizenship despite their presence in Myanmar for many generations. And he found widespread favour among other Buddhists in the country, who turned him into a hero and celebrity.

Islamophobia, some of it exported to Asia from the American media, is now a growing cancer throughout the region. Similar anti-Muslim movements targeting marginalized minorities are afoot in Sri Lanka, and perhaps Thailand as well. It may be that the terrible Rohingya refugee emergency is only the first in a series of violent mass attacks by Buddhist majorities against their neighbors. The rhetorical parallels to nativist movements in the United States are striking: talk about suspicious outsiders, unassimilable foreigners, criminal aliens, teeming hoards that pose economic and religious threats to the rightful majority, and official and extra-legal actions to control, displace, terrorize, and eliminate whole communities. But rather than being the targets of such hate as they have sometimes been in North America, it is Buddhists themselves who are carrying out these campaigns in Southeast Asia.

Buddhism and the dispossessed

As we can see, we are faced with a huge and growing number of crises, almost all of them due to human behaviour and choices. It's human actions that have led us to this point: human choices to kill, to exclude, to exploit, to hoard, to pollute, to over-consume, to turn our backs on the needs of one another. Whether carried out against Buddhists or by Buddhists, or by others in other situations, these choices are rooted in the three mental poisons identified by the Buddha: greed, hatred, and ignorance.

The Buddhist analysis of the world and the human situation is often characterized as pessimistic. Given the very real nature of the widespread suffering in the world, we might say that it is simply sadly realistic. Buddhism recognizes that we inhabit a world of insecurity and suffering, known as samsara, the cycle of life and death. The Buddha's famous Fire Sermon pulls no punches. As he is recorded to have preached, "Monks, everything is burning. And what is this everything that is burning? The eye is burning, forms are burning... the ear is burning... the nose is burning... the tongue is burning... the body is burning... the mind is burning... also whatever is felt as pleasant or painful or neither-painful-nor-pleasant... that too is burning. Burning with what? Burning with the fire of greed, with the fire of hate, with the fire of ignorance. I say it is burning with birth, aging, and death, with sorrows, with lamentations, with pains, with griefs, with despairs."

These three fundamental sources of suffering—greed, hatred, and ignorance—are characterized as poisons because they taint the minds of all unawakened beings and contribute to a ceaseless cycle of misery. They underlie not only our great evils of war and oppression, but the thousand banal acts of unskillfulness that we each commit daily, adding to the creation of a world that is so much less than it could be.

Buddhism offers a dire analysis of the human condition and the state of this world we have produced. But it doesn't stop there.

Buddhist insights and concepts also offer hope for a better way. Buddhism focuses on suffering precisely because it is a system designed to eliminate suffering from our lives. Buddhism is a system meant to bring about an end to greed, hatred, and ignorance through training in wisdom, compassion, and moral clarity. As such, it can identify the underlying causes that lead to the crises we are discussing here, and potentially provide guidance on how to deal with them.

The most foundational insights of the Buddha's teaching are that all things are impermanent, that everything arises due to interconnected causes and conditions, and that our actions have inevitable effects in the world. It's because of these facts that we are confronted by the incredibly complex interwoven crises that I have been describing so far. But the same observations of the Buddha also mean that the situations we face aren't permanent, that even the worst conditions can be improved, that individual and collective actions will be productive, and that making even small positive efforts will have a ripple effect that subtly affects the whole world.

Buddhism isn't a singular thing, really. It's a large collection of many different traditions, with different languages, iconography, and practices. But within this diversity there is something central that they all share: the goal of eliminating suffering. In my understanding of the Buddhist path, this transformation of suffering into peace must take place both internally and externally. Internally, we must recognize the role of our own minds in producing our suffering and that of others. Buddhism provides a huge range of tools and techniques that have been refined over millennia for the blossoming of insight, lovingkindness, and equanimity.

Externally, we must have proper conditions of security and comfort to practice the arts of awakening. Buddhist technologies of meditation, study, analysis, moral refinement, and so on can only reach their greatest potentials when practitioners are enabled to pursue them through access to adequate education, food, water, shelter, and community support, and the absence of the dire sufferings caused by violence, depravation, displacement, environmental danger, and oppression. Furthermore, because we are all interconnected, I can't achieve the genuine lasting peace and happiness that

Buddhism aims at unless you achieve it as well. So long as anyone suffers, I too will be subject to suffering. To complete the Buddhist path, therefore, we must address both the internal and external sources of suffering. In other words, we need transformations of society just as much as transformations of ourselves. Becoming aware of the sources of forced migration, climate change, homelessness, and other pressing concerns, and working to solve these problems, is therefore just as faithful to the Buddhist tradition as chanting, reading sutras, and listening to Dharma talks. Ultimately, we will need all of these and more if we are to reduce suffering in our world and ourselves.

Buddhism has a long history with ideas of homelessness, security, and insecurity. The birth of Buddhism began when Siddhartha Gautama abandoned his home to seek religious answers to the problem of suffering. The formal name for a Buddhist monk or nun is a *bhikshu* or *bhikshuni*, which literally means beggar, and the process of ordination is called *shukke tokudo*, literally "home-leaving to reach the other shore." The primary act of Buddhism is described as taking refuge, meaning that the Buddha, his teaching, and the community of practitioners are understood as refuges that provide security in a turbulent world. From this perspective, all Buddhists are theoretically refugees, as they recognize the turmoil of existence and go to Buddhism to reach peace and contentment.

But it is easy to take these ideas too far, and assign them meanings or significance they didn't have, historically speaking. While all Buddhists may be refugees in an abstract sense, this hardly compares to the struggles of forcibly displaced persons, and while monks and nuns may be home-leavers, their voluntary hardships pale in comparison to the unwanted suffering of the genuinely unhoused. In fact, the Buddhist monk is not really homeless at all: rather, the newly ordained bhikshu or bhikshuni enters a new family and receives a new, better home than they had before. Indeed, Buddhist monks receive a new surname, Shaku, the name of the Buddha, Shakyamuni. In other words, they're adopted into the family of the Buddha and are welcomed into the ultimate refuge, the most superior home: that of the protected and revered Buddhist community, known by the Sanskrit term *sangha*.

The sangha was designed as a sheltered alternate society, which embodied the vision of the ideal social world. In contrast to our chaotic normal lives, the sangha was ordered and orderly. Rather than competition and struggle, it was based on sharing of resources, communal support, and non-acquisitiveness. It was open to women, outcastes, and others for whom there was no status in normal society. The sangha was a place of safety: it was illegal to harm monks and nuns, and attacks on the sangha were believed to generate terrible karma that would haunt the perpetrator for lifetimes to come. Monks could not be conscripted into the army or used for other slave labour purposes. The sangha received the necessities for life from the supporting lay community, and in turn they dedicated themselves to inner and outer transformation of the world, through moral behaviour, ritual, teaching, acts of charity, and mental cultivation.

In premodern Asia, the sangha became a crucial form of social support for the needy. It was a home for orphans, widows, refugees, and others without social security. Those who entered the monastery were ensured a basic subsistence, a place to live, a network of support, and access to education. Not surprisingly, it was popular in Japan for retired aristocrats to join the sangha following a regime change, as this placed them beyond the reach of reprisals by their rivals. Buddhist monasteries often served as hostels or dormitories for travelers, students, and the temporarily displaced. They provided loans to peasants and entrepreneurs at low or no interest rates, and raised funds for hospitals, bridges, wells, roads, and other essential forms of infrastructure that especially impacted the poor.

This sense that Buddhism offered security in a tumultuous world, and that the sangha provided an alternative society and mode of life, eventually reached its highest degree in the Pure Land tradition. This form of Buddhism focuses on the story of entering the realm of happiness, which has been purified of suffering and pain, as a way of understanding nirvana. The land of purity is created by Amida Buddha, the embodiment of ultimate wisdom and compassion, as a place where anyone can go to find safety, rest, and instruction in the way to Buddhahood, away from the dangers of ordinary life. As such, the Pure Land is a vision of the perfect world, the way in which society should be run if only we were able to conquer the poisons that hold us back. It is a place where everyone is welcome, where there is no war or evil, and all receive adequate clothing, food, protection, and education. Pure Land became the most popular form of Buddhism in East Asia, and not surprisingly it was especially prominent during times of war, famine, epidemics, and other disasters.

This idea of Pure Land as the way to refuge and security is most famously embodied in the Chinese Buddhist parable of the white path, created by the master Shandao. This was a favourite story of Shinran, who related and commented on it in his writings. For him, it was more than a mere figment of the imagination, for it described his experiences in terms that felt accurate and real. In the parable, a traveler is lost in the wilderness. Bandits and wild animals appear and attack him, and he runs from them until he comes to a riverbank. The channel is filled by two rivers, one of churning waves and the other of raging flames. There is a narrow white path between the two rivers, but it seems impossible to cross over successfully. Terrified, exhausted, and threatened from all sides, the traveler is in great peril, but at just that moment the voice of Shakyamuni Buddha comes to him, telling him that he can make it, and he hears the voice of Amida Buddha calling from the other side, promising that he won't be destroyed. The traveler flees over the white path, entering the peaceful land of the Buddha, where he lives happily ever after.

This parable, of course, depicts the Pure Land understanding of our human condition, which is fundamentally about the search for a secure home as we traverse this world of troubles. The river of water is the forces of greed, while the river of fire is the burning hate and resentment we experience in ourselves and others. The land of desolation is this contentious, unawakened world where we suffer and are under constant threat. As Shinran explains, the white path is shinjin, the trusting heart that abandons self-striving and turns toward the collective liberation brought about by relying on the Primal Vow. The other shore is the Pure Land, the goal of Buddhism depicted in the form of a place of safety and protection for all after the suffering of wandering and exile. It is the function of Amida

Buddha, "the ultimate shelter," to offer freedom from mundane and existential suffering through the refuge of the Pure Land.

Taking Action

The profound inclusivity of the Jodo Shinshu way helped to turn Shinran's understanding into the largest school of Buddhism in Japan, and therefore, not surprisingly, the most popular one among the Japanese diaspora in North America and Hawai'i as well. While I find them especially well-expressed in Shinran's writings, I also encounter similar ideas about compassion for others, caring for those in need, offering shelter, medicine, food, and protection to suffering people, and working to build a better world in the teachings of other forms of Buddhism too. And as I reflect further, I notice that Christianity, Judaism, Islam, and many other religions likewise share these ideals. Therefore, I believe we are most faithful to our cherished traditions precisely when we apply them to the problems of those around us.

The question, then, is what we can do to respond to the tremendous suffering of the displaced and dispossessed in the world today? The first thing to be done is education. This begins by following the news, seeking information about the troubles in the world, and trying to understand the intersecting causes that lead to exile, environmental destruction, incarceration, mass migration, and homelessness. The Buddhist insight into the interconnectedness of all things will be necessary to confront the challenges of the 21st century and beyond. Pain and suffering over there result in pain and suffering here. Waste of resources here results in pollution everywhere. Racist posturing by politicians and media figures contributes to oppression and genocide at home and abroad, while military actions in foreign lands soon enough result in displaced innocents at one's own doorstep in need of care. Protectionism and nativism are farces in a globalized, electronically and physically connected world that refuses to respect whatever borders we try to impose on it.

Beyond simple education, the next step is to open our hearts to those who suffer. This can be frightening and painful work. The magnitude of suffering in the world today, or even in our own city, is easily overwhelming. The impulse is strong to look away, to shut down our feelings, protect ourselves, and turn our backs. It is difficult to struggle with the fact that we live on stolen land, that children starve while we eat in front of the TV, that entire nations have been destroyed while we worked and played, and that no matter how hard we try to help, more destruction will surely happen. Yet to give up is to abandon the Buddha's quest for an end to suffering. Turning away makes a mockery of Shinran's all-embracing teaching.

Once we have begun to notice the suffering of the world, and even more importantly, begun to care, it's time to follow-up with action. I am under no illusions that any of us can truly eliminate suffering in its entirety from samsara. But we do all have the power to make a difference, small or large.

Let me give you an example. At the Toronto Buddhist Church, we have a Sunday School called the Kids Sangha. In 2015, the kids had been hearing about the plight of Syrian refugee children on the news. So, they announced that they were holding a series of bake sales, and they donated the funds to Plan Canada. Plan Canada is a service that creates safe spaces for injured and ailing children to recover, provides mental health and emotional support for children and their parents, tries to improve access to education in protected learning environments, and advocates for greater public and private support for vulnerable children and families. For the adults at the temple, we were humbled by this initiative that the children took all on their own, so we began a fundraising campaign too, which the Canadian federal government matched.

As a minority religion in North America and Hawai'i, I think it is often wise for Buddhists to partner with other religious and civic groups. We are stronger together, and other groups or religions may have experience, infrastructure, or funds that exceed our own. For example, my wife lived in Syria for over a year and half back in the 1990s, and when the Syrian civil war began, she was distraught at the destruction of her old neighborhood and the suffering of her friends. She began working with the refugee task force of our local Unitarian Universalist church—in fact, for a time she became the primary leader of the group. Through this connection our family has been able to help bring eight Syrian refugees to safety in Ontario.

The first was a transgender woman who faced extreme discrimination and serious danger even within the refugee population itself. Next, we sponsored a family of seven: mom, dad, three children, and two grandparents. With our help, they rented a house, the dad got a job, and the mom took computer lessons. One of the most moving parts for me was about their 12-year-old daughter. Growing up as a refugee in Saudi Arabia, she was barred from learning to drive because she is female. But once she came to Canada, she began taking flying lessons, and she dreams of being a pilot when she grows up. I can't think of a better possible metaphor for the freedom that refugee children experience when we take the time to care and get involved.

Improving the lives of eight refugees doesn't end the misery that so many still face. But you can't tell me that it doesn't matter, that it doesn't contribute. I look at these young people, flying and growing, and I know that our every effort matters more than we will ever understand. They are the living embodiment of the old maxim to think globally and act locally.

If we think about it, the process of involvement is more of a cycle than a straightforward path. While pursuing action, we also continue to deepen our education, widen our compassion, and seek partnerships with others. Each step reinforces the others: the experience of helping others teaches us much through trial and error, motivates us to keep working, and often leads to encounters with new partners.

Let me give you some examples of what I mean. The Jodo Shinshu tradition has two main branches, commonly known as Nishi and Higashi. In North America each year, ministers from the Nishi and Higashi organizations get together for a joint education series known as WeHope. In 2017, the WeHope seminars were not focused on Buddhism, as they typically are. Instead, the ministers spent their time learning about Islam from local Muslim leaders, and jointly visited a mosque. This was done because they recognized that Muslims face strong suspicion and discrimination in our society, that a large portion of the refugees and immigrants seeking entrance to the United States are Muslim, and that as Buddhists we aren't automatically equipped to understand Islam, Muslims, or the problems they face.

Studying Islam with members of both Buddhist organizations and learning face-to-face from real Muslims provided both education and the chance to deepen compassion for the challenges faced by our Muslim neighbors. It strengthened the partnership between Nishi and Higashi because ministers were able to reflect on the challenges and discrimination our own organizations have experienced, and it laid the foundations for temple ministers to correct misinformation about Islam among their members and lead them in compassionate outreach to Muslim refugees in need. In Hawai'i, there have been similar efforts undertaken by several Buddhist women's organizations that have met with Muslim women to talk story, clear up their misunderstandings, and build bridges between communities that elsewhere in the world are unfortunately at each other's throats.

Perhaps the most moving example of these partnerships was the fast-breaking event held at Senshin Buddhist Temple in South Central Los Angeles, in 2002. A year after the deadly Al-Qaeda attacks of September 11, 2001, the American invasion of Afghanistan, and violence against Muslims and others by racist vigilantes, the National Coalition for Redress/Reparations organized breaking-the-fast events during Ramadan. A mixed group of Jodo Shinshu Buddhists and Muslims gathered in Senshin's *hondo* (sanctuary), while Rev. Masao Kodani led them in chanting a Buddhist sutra. Then Kamau Ayubbi, a young man of Black, Japanese, and white background who grew up attending Senshin, rose. He'd become a Muslim in college and had just been appointed an imam. Now in this hall where he'd sang and chanted as a Buddhist child, the Muslim call to prayer rolled out of him and across the pews where Buddhists and Muslims sat in solidarity. Then they enjoyed a meal together, as friends and neighbors.

Another positive example is Buddhist participation in the Family Promise program in Hawai'i. Family Promise provides services to families in danger of becoming unsheltered or who are experiencing homelessness. Perhaps the heart of their operation is their emergency housing program, in which local congregations provide meals and space at their temple or church where an unsheltered family can sleep overnight for a week. Family Promise also provides access to case workers, assistance with housing searches, job training, and education. Several Jodo Shinshu temples are involved either as emergency housing sites or as financial supporters, and other Family Promise partners include Catholic, Protestant, Mormon, Jewish, Muslim, and Unitarian Universalist congregations. This sort of inter-faith social service is a perfect example of the sort of coalition building that is crucial for tackling our major social problems. Because homelessness and other displacements are communal problems, it will take communal responses to solve them.

These are primarily examples of local direct action, since that's often where we can have the biggest impact, and importantly, where we can most easily see the positive outcomes from our work, which is necessary for preventing burnout and sustaining our well of compassion. However, many problems must be approached at larger scales. For example, when the withdrawal of American troops from Vietnam in 1975 led to a swell in refugees, the Canadian, Hawaiian, and mainland American Jodo Shinshu bishops issued a joint statement:

> In the past month over 200,000 Viet Nam refugees have fled from the Communist takeover of South Viet Nam and have sought refuge in the United States. They have emigrated with just the bare necessities of life into an environment totally different in language, culture, and religion. Under such circumstances they naturally face fears and anxieties for the future welfare of themselves as well as their families. We can readily understand their hardships because Japanese Americans suffered a similar fate during World War II in the trying period of evacuation, relocation, and resettlement. The plight of the refugees is even more difficult, complicated by cultural differences and communication problems. We, therefore, call upon all Americans to give all the necessary assistance in

> the resettlement of these displaced people. We further urge all Buddhists to extend the hand of compassion in helping our Viet Nam brothers and sisters in building new lives—in obtaining jobs, homes, and places of worship.

The Buddhist Churches of America immediately organized an Office of Refugee Settlement, which placed twenty-five refugees with temple families in California. The Office held a clothing drive that generated multiple truckloads of donations for refugees at army camps. BCA temples contributed thousands of dollars, and distributed Buddhist altars, *malas* (Buddhist rosary beads), and images to the refugees. Ministers made pastoral visits to refugees at army camps and conducted Buddhist services. The Office of Refugee Settlement closed when the two-year sponsorships ended in 1977, but funds continued to be raised and donated. The 1979 Cambodian refugee crisis led the BCA to reactivate their Social Welfare Committee. Its first action was to establish the BCA Cambodian Relief Fund, which ran until 1981 and sent over $31,000 to UNICEF Cambodian Relief, the World Fellowship of Buddhists, International Rescue Committee, and Operation Survival.

The size of challenges that we face today means that many will need to be tackled at the international level or on scales impossible for a local person, family, or temple to handle. This is where government action comes in, and in a democracy that means pressuring our elected officials to act with compassion and intelligence. Jodo Shinshu Buddhists in North America and Hawai'i have a long history of civic engagement for the betterment of society. Bishops, ministers, and lay leaders have been speaking their mind for over a century, starting with support for striking sugar cane workers in the first years of the 20th century. Issues they've made public statements on include opposition to school prayer and the death penalty, support for the 1964 Civil Rights Act, the need for action on climate change, personal choice in abortion decisions, and more. Voting, marching, protesting, writing to your representatives, and in some cases running for office yourself are all religious actions when carried out for the benefit of others. Likewise, donating money to non-governmental organizations and para-church relief funds is an authentic way to do our part to live our best principles.

One of the most shameful actions of the Trump administration was the ban on travel by citizens of several majority Muslim nations, which was initially combined with a ban on nearly all refugees. This travel ban did nothing to increase America's security, while betraying the country's legacy as a beacon of hope and justice for those who suffer around the world. It was heartening, though, that opposition to the ban was led especially by Asian American groups that understand the connection between the WWII incarceration of Japanese Americans and today's anti-Muslim policies. One of the most vocal of these was Tsuru for Solidarity, whose cofounders and many prominent local leaders include a significant number of Jodo Shinshu Buddhists. They demonstrated one of the clear ways in which we should be responding to world events: by educating ourselves about the problems and their causes; linking them with the compassion we've developed through our own experiences with suffering and injustice; and demanding better.

Pressure can also be applied internationally. Both before and after the Myanmar genocide against its Rohingya Muslim minority, Buddhist voices around the world denounced their marginalization. Buddhist Global Relief, based in New York City, and the Buddhist Humanitarian Project, based in Berkeley, California, have collected money to provide supplies to the Rohingya refugees, marshaling opposition to the government's policies, and educating people about the oppression. The efforts made by young Burmese American Buddhists on social media to bring world attention to the sufferings of the Rohingya, denounce the use of Buddhism as a cover for atrocities, and attempt to steer Myanmar onto a better path were particularly touching.

In summary, our world is wracked by intertwined, complex problems of insecurity and displacement at the global, national, and local levels. Our daily actions contribute to many of these woes, and collectively our societies have not responded sufficiently to deal with the profound challenges of the 21st century. Jodo Shinshu Buddhists in particular should be mindful of the suffering of refugees, persecuted immigrants, and the unhoused. Given our concern for suffering, our understanding of interconnection, the struggles of our founders, the all-embracing nature of our philosophy, and the experiences of insecurity and exclusion that our own communities have faced, to do otherwise would be to betray our heritage. I feel we should forcefully denounce hatred and oppression wherever they are found, especially when carried out in the name of Buddhism, and we should partner with our neighbors in other faiths to seek solutions and shared community.

5

Principles for Engaged Shin Buddhism

QUESTIONS DRIVING THIS BOOK: what must Pure Land Buddhism, especially the Jodo Shinshu school, do to contribute to the reduction of suffering in the world, especially as caused or heightened by social ills such as discrimination, poverty, war, and climate change? What are some elements of the tradition that can inspire or inform our efforts at reducing harm in the world?

From Shinran's unique and penetrating understanding of the meaning of Amida Buddha's story, we can identify six specific principles that may guide Jodo Shinshu Buddhist engagement with life and work to transform suffering. These principles derive from Shinran's teaching across his many writings, but especially from *Tannisho*, one of the most treasured of all Japanese texts. It's a collection of conversations and teachings by Shinran and his close disciple Yuien-bo.

Pure Land Buddhism shares much with other forms of Buddhism and, in many places, it is integrated with other Buddhisms to form part of the general matrix of Buddhist practice and thought. Among the Pure Land schools and more general approaches, Jodo Shinshu stands out both due to its size and due to its unique interpretation of Buddhist practice. For Shin Buddhism, the key to all authentic Buddhist practice is gratitude. And this central value of gratitude is also what provides the link between Shin Buddhist practice in general and religiously motivated action to improve society and protect the natural environment.

Many forms of Buddhism, especially those associated with the Mahayana tradition, teach that the universe in its truest reality is liberated, spontaneous, and pure. Unfortunately, though, we don't actually experience it in this way. We are self-centred and self-attached, and this attitude leads us to create suffering for ourselves and others. To wake us up to this painful egocentricity and point us back to the underlying purity of things as they are, the story of the Pure Land has been handed down and cherished over scores of generations. It is with this story, then, that we must begin in our assessment of Pure Land Buddhism's social potentiality.

The story of the Pure Land is recorded in the *Larger Pure Land Sutra*, a scripture ascribed to the Buddha, who lived in India 2,500 years ago. Once upon a time, there was an unnamed king. He was just another entitled man hoarding privilege and money, until he encountered a buddha, who woke him up to the truth and demonstrated that profound wisdom and compassion were possible. Awakened to the meaninglessness of his selfish life, he abandoned power and wealth to work toward the liberation of all beings from pain and suffering. At this moment he became a bodhisattva and received the sacred name Dharmakara, meaning "[Inexhaustible] Storehouse of Dharma."

The method that Dharmakara took was investigation. Tutored by the buddha, he examined all the cultures, countries, and worlds of the universe, peering into their positive and negative aspects. He examined how every person—good and bad—lived, and how their various lifestyles and karmic situations brought about suffering or happiness. He investigated the vows and practices of the various buddhas who lived in these lands, determining the strong and weak points in their quests to aid others. Then he contemplated these things for a long, long time, turning them over in his mind until he had fully understood how to bring about his plan for universal liberation. Among the things he learned was what conditions are necessary to develop deep wisdom and compassion, and what circumstances prevent people from experiencing happiness or developing spiritual insight.

When he had fully analyzed everything, Dharmakara put his plan into action. He determined to cultivate a society and environment in which suffering was eradicated and all beings lived harmoniously, without suffering or delusion. He would welcome all people throughout the universe into his community, where they would be taken care of and trained to develop wisdom and compassion equal to the buddhas. This community of people, animals, plants, water, and land would be nirvana itself expressed in the form of a loving sangha, and all who joined would be liberated from their pain and ignorance. Because of its perfection, it is known as the Realm of Bliss, the Land of Happiness, or the Pure Land.

The bodhisattva Dharmakara established many vows to fortify his intention and make explicit the nature of this pure land of bliss and happiness. The most important aspect of all these vows is that Dharmakara staked his liberation on the liberation of others. His vows are all phrased in the following manner: “If, for countless eons to come, I should not become a great benefactor and save all the destitute and afflicted everywhere, may I not attain buddhahood.” In other words, if I can’t endlessly help the poor and sick, I refuse to become a buddha. It is to help everyone that I am pursuing buddhahood.

Having made his resolve, Dharmakara practiced for an inconceivably long time to fulfill his vows. He worked with his mind until he had eliminated greed, hatred, and cruelty, the qualities that most oppose the Pure Land way. He freed his mind of falsehoods, approached others with tenderness and kindness, and spoke to them in harmony with their deepest thoughts. He realized the deepest truths of interdependence and inner togetherness, renounced wealth, and trained in generosity, ethics, patience, perseverance, meditation, and wisdom. Life after life he was reborn to continue his training and plumb ever deeper into the realities of human living and suffering. He was born as a rich person and poor one, learning the needs and karmic conditions of each. He made offerings and accumulated vast merit, until he was able to complete the path.

Dharmakara thus became Amida Buddha. Amida means “infinite, boundless, endless.” It is a Japanese rendition of two Sanskrit names, Amitabha and Amitayus, which mean “infinite light” and “boundless life.” These in turn mean “infinite enlightening wisdom” and “endless life-supporting compassion.” These are the nature of what Amida is: Amida is infinite enlightening wisdom and endless life-supporting compassion.

The Pure Land is Dharmakara’s vision of the perfect society and environment. It thus provides us a template for how we should try to conduct ourselves, and what the best society would be like. The forty-eight core vows of the *Larger Pure Land Sutra* reveal what this vision is for Pure Land Buddhists. Put simply, those vows are that in the perfect society:

- No one will suffer (vows 1-2)
- No one will experience discrimination due to appearance (vows 3-4, 21, 27)
- No one will experience physical or mental impairment (vows 5-9, 28-30, 40-41, 46)
- No one will have to worry about their body (vows 10, 26, 33)
- Amida's wisdom and compassion will be infinite, and all will share in it (vows 11-15, 19-20, 22, 25, 34, 36-37, 44-45, 47-48)
- People will speak of good, not evil (vows 16-17)
- Without hardship, all will be freed from suffering (vow 18)
- Everyone will have freedom of movement (vows 23, 42)
- There will be no poverty (vow 24)
- The environment will be pure and wondrous (vows 31-32)
- There will be no gender discrimination (vow 35)
- Everyone will have sufficient clothing (vow 38)
- Everyone will be happy (vow 39)
- No one will be disadvantaged (vow 43)

Or, put conversely, these vows reveal the sorts of sources of suffering that Amida Buddha seeks to eliminate—ignorance, attachment, poverty, lack of clothes or housing, confinement, disability, environmental disruption, and racial, gender, and similar discriminations. The implications for social action should be clear from this list.

This is the sacred story from which Pure Land Buddhism derives its meaning and values. Across the great variety of Buddhisms that employ Pure Land ideas and motifs, the story of Dharmakara's compassionate building of the Land of Bliss is the central unifying element. It is what gave Shinran strength to endure persecution, exile, hardship, and heartbreak over his long life of Buddhist teaching.

While all Pure Land Buddhists affirm this story, there are differences in how various schools interpret it and put it into practice. Shinran's approach to practice is arguably the most radical in

Buddhist history. For Shinran, the only fully authentic religious practice is the expression of thankfulness. Meditation, prayer, ritual, mantra, and all the other common elements of Buddhist practice are too often based on self-striving or a desire to get a return on one's investment. But the self is precisely the source of suffering in the first place, and ego-tainted efforts are useless for true emancipation. Gratitude alone is based on non-striving, on awareness of benefits already received. The efforts of Dharmakara to establish the Pure Land and secure our liberation are the foundation of gratitude in Jodo Shinshu. From this we expand our view to become aware of all the things that contribute to our lives and awakening. We express our thankfulness though saying the nembutsu, Namo Amida Butsu: Thank you, Amida Buddha. Thank you, Infinite Light and Boundless Life. Thank you, Endless Wisdom and All-Embracing Compassion.

First Principle
Amida Embraces All Beings Unconditionally

In *Tannisho*, Shinran states, "The Primal Vow of Amida makes no distinction between people young and old, good and evil." The Primal Vow is vow eighteen, the vow that *everyone* can enter the Pure Land and be freed from suffering. This great vow is not based on distinctions between people. It isn't a gift given to the good, the rich, the mighty, the enfranchised. Nor is it a prize or reward achieved by the diligent, the hard-working, the insightful, the pious. It is made for absolutely everyone. It's made for men and for women, and for those who are nonbinary or otherwise complicate or transcend this dualism. It is made for straight people and for gay people, and for all possible inclinations toward love. It is made for Black people and white people and Asian people, and for all people of whatever race, ethnicity, or culture exist. The Pure Land is for all of us.

Amida Buddha completely refuses to discriminate against anyone whatsoever. From this, we learn that discrimination is wrong and must be resisted. Prejudice must not be permitted in our sanghas, and it must not be accepted in society. Rather, we must recognize our solidarity with all people and all living things, and work to promote this solidarity. This solidarity arises from the fact that we are all equally embraced, and because all beings have been intimately related to us since the beginningless past. As Shinran says in *Tannisho*, "All sentient beings, without exception, have been our parents and brothers and sisters in the course of countless lives in the many states of existence." He makes this point during a discussion about whether one should say the nembutsu for one's parents (ancestor veneration is a venerable East Asian Buddhist practice). Shinran rejects it because it's too constricted: there isn't a single being who hasn't been our parents and siblings in the past. Every person you meet, everyone you pass on the street, is your kin. Just as you would not tolerate discrimination against your current mother or brother, you must not discriminate against others or allow anyone to languish under the oppression of prejudice.

To embrace others unconditionally is difficult. Only the Buddha truly achieves it, but nevertheless we strive to emulate that Great Compassion and do our best to accept others. An example of this is the long history of same-sex marriage in Jodo Shinshu temples, which I noted in chapter two. The very first known Buddhist same-sex marriage in history happened at the Buddhist Church of San Francisco in the early 1970s, approximately fifty years ago. In 2010 the Hawaiian Jodo Shinshu temples explained the basis for this accepting attitude:

> WHEREAS, the Dharma (universal teachings) provides guidance on how to live mindfully with an awareness of universal compassion which embraces and uplifts each and every person; and
>
> WHEREAS, in order to truly realize universal compassion, we need to cultivate a profound sense of responsibility for the welfare of all beings; and
>
> WHEREAS, the Buddhist ideal of universal compassion does not discriminate between good and evil, young and old, rich and poor, gay and straight; and
>
> WHEREAS, Buddhism affirms the inherent worth and dignity of all persons independent of gender; and

> WHEREAS, families today are composed of many combinations and what connects individuals as a family is a conscious commitment to share in the responsibilities of life; and...
>
> WHEREAS, Shinran Shonin, the founder of Shin Buddhism, affirmed the inherent equality among all people whose lives are karmically (causally) bound and interconnected by teaching that the great Wisdom and Compassion of Amida (ultimate reality) embraces all beings equally and unconditionally without exception...
>
> NOW, THEREFORE, BE IT RESOLVED, that the Honpa Hongwanji Mission of Hawai'i, a Shin Buddhist organization, affirms that same-gender couples should have access to equal rights and quality of life as conferred by legally recognized marriage....

We have performed weddings for male couples and lesbians, for transgender people, for bisexuals, for polyamorists—love is love, and we've accommodated all its beautiful forms without conflict. How could we do otherwise? Amida Buddha embraces everyone, so there is no possible foundation upon which we could build a coherent argument against recognizing the worth of others, whether they seem similar or different from us.

This universal embrace extends beyond human beings, we should note. All living things are included in Amida Buddha's compassion. We can see this in simple acts of comradeship with the natural world. For instance, in Winnipeg Jodo Shinshu minister Rev. Fred Ulrich often conducted funerals for trees blown down by the wind. There's no specific requirement to do so in Jodo Shinshu doctrine. But he felt compassion for these great beings whose lives were cut short, and spontaneously provided them with funeral rites as an expression of his sympathy. Wearing his black Buddhist robes and chanting sutras, he reminded the trees that we care for them and apologized for human actions that contributed to their deaths.

Second Principle
Even the Good are Saved, So of Course the Evil are Saved

More than 700 years ago, Shinran said that "Even a good person attains birth in the Pure Land, so it goes without saying that an evil person will." This is Shinran's most important teaching in *Tannisho*, and it once again demonstrates his radicalness.

Buddhists of the past and of Shinran's time taught that Amida Buddha's power and compassion were so great that even an *evil* person attains birth in the Pure Land through the buddha's power (even though they hardly deserved it). Their real point was that therefore we can automatically be confident that *good* people go to the Pure Land (since they actually do deserve it). In other words, people were told if they obeyed the authorities, followed the rules, donated to the monasteries, and did other good practices, they were certain to be reborn through the Pure Land. After all, even *evil* people get to go there, at least theoretically. So, be good, and get into the Pure Land.

Shinran completely rejected this logic. For Shinran, the Great Compassion does not exist for the so-called good people alone. Indeed, they're not even its primary concern. Therefore, Shinran recognized that this venerable Buddhist teaching needed to be rephrased to reveal the full purpose of Amida Buddha's Primal Vow.

Shinran taught that *even a good person* receives rebirth through the Pure Land way, so therefore it goes without saying that *of course evil people* do so. Shinran understood that Amida Buddha, the Great Compassion, exists to liberate all beings from our suffering. That is the only reason that the Pure Land exists, to be an engine for our liberation, all of us. It is not a heaven for Amida Buddha to bliss out in; it is not a reward for those who somehow earn it; it is not a gated community or a VIP hangout behind a velvet rope. It is the means that Dharmakara came up with whereby to liberate all beings from suffering.

Thus, Amida Buddha cares about the fact that someone is suffering, not about whether they're supposedly good or evil. Indeed, those who are *labeled* evil are typically the ones who suffer the most. Therefore, Shinran teaches that it is those who need the most help whom Amida liberates *first*: those who suffer the most, and those who are excluded from elite approaches to Buddhism. They are the first priority of Great Compassion.

As I explained in chapter two, "evil" is often a label that society attaches to the unwanted and marginalized. For example, politicians often target immigrants, especially so-called "illegal immigrants," for attack. Politicians paint such people as criminals, rapists, welfare drags, job-stealers, drug dealers, and more, and then pledge to protect voters from such evil threats. Likewise, Muslims have endured decades of xenophobic targeting by politicians, the media, and racist vigilantes. For millennia various patriarchal religions and cultures have taught that women are somehow inherently sinful or dangerous, and used this to justify controlling and oppressing them. To be called evil is often a sign not of one's lack of morality, but of the lack of value that dominant society assigns to someone in your group.

Into this situation, the Great Compassion arrives as a disruptive force. Rather than those who are already given the relative means to reduce their suffering, or who are privileged to escape the suffering caused by prejudice and oppression, Amida Buddha's vow is especially directed toward those who are called evil. Thus the "evil" and suffering must be the first object of our compassionate action in the world. When we seek to positively impact our world, our first question should not be "who deserves to be helped" or even "what can I do to help?" It should be "who is suffering, and how?" All engaged Jodo Shinshu work arises from the facts of suffering, and is a response to those facts. It's not an ego-based wish to feel good about oneself or to act as a savior, nor is it about accumulating merit or receiving distinction. Following from Amida Buddha's example, we look to see where there is great suffering, and we act to alleviate it as best we can. All lives contain suffering, and there is work to do in all areas for everyone. But the greatest sufferers—the oppressed, the marginalized, the excluded, the disenfranchised—must be our primary concern.

An example of this is prison ministry, which takes place in some of the most soul-crushing environments imaginable. In Japan, Jodo Shinshu Buddhists were the first to initiate formal prison chaplaincy, and from the later part of the 19th century through the end of World War II, Jodo Shinshu ministers were practically the only Buddhists working in the prisons. Thus, it's natural that the first Buddhist prison ministry in the mainland United States was carried out by a member of the Buddhist Churches of America, Rev. Hogen Fujimoto. He conducted regular correspondence with prisoners and held services in California prisons starting in the 1960s, such as San Quentin. Rev. Fujimoto encountered racism by the inmates (few of whom were Asian American), suspicion by guards, and the threat of violence, but he took comfort in the responses of the prisoners themselves, whose thirst for the Dharma was undeniable. As he saw the Dharma operate in their lives as it had in his own, he widened his activities, starting programs in various prisons and corresponding with inmates across the country.

And his efforts bore fruit for those in the hell realm of the prison system. Though he couldn't change the entire system, with its many sufferings and injustices, he did lighten the lives of many people. One of these was a Jodo Shinshu Buddhist of Mexican American background, Fred Cruz, who tried to share the Dharma materials that Rev. Fujimoto provided with other inmates in the Texas prison system. But the guards confiscated his Buddhist books and threw him in solitary confinement for months, where he received only water and two pieces of bread per day. Cruz meticulously wrote out a lawsuit on toilet paper against the prison. It was repeatedly denied by local judges, but he persevered all the way to the Supreme Court, which ruled in 1972 that his constitutional rights had been violated. This judgment established for the first time that the practice of Buddhism in American prisons was legal and protected, and became the bedrock upon which subsequent prison ministry by Buddhists of various traditions relied. Cruz also applied the lessons he learned from his court battles to help Black Muslims pursue their own religious rights in the prison system.

A more general example of this principle of giving special attention to those who suffer the most—in a non-Buddhist context, this time—is the Black Lives Matter movement. To me, Black Lives Matter is nembutsu, because it tells those who are said to be evil that they are embraced. All people matter, but Black people have been called evil, told their lives don't matter, and received centuries of crushing oppression and violence due to the belief that they are worth less or worthless. That's why the Black Lives Matter movement is necessary: because some people have suffered much more than others, and their lives have not been affirmed. And that is why it is a type of nembutsu to say "Black lives matter." It is a way of rejecting the standard social logic and redirecting our attention from the supposed centre to the margins, where it belongs. This is truly the spirit of Shinran's dictum.

Third Principle
I Too Am a Foolish Being

In discussing political competitions, social justice, environmental issues, and similar matters, there is always a strong tendency to fall into an us vs. them, right vs. wrong mentality of deep polarization, self-aggrandizement, and vilification of those who disagree. This is a natural but regrettable phenomenon, since rarely are we all right or our "opponents" all wrong, and our goal as Pure Land Buddhists is peace, harmony, and liberation with all people. Excessive anger and hatred of others defeats our actual purpose, and pushes us off the way of Great Compassion.

Shinran was a person of deep personal conviction, so deep that he defied the emperor and the feudal Buddhist establishment, and received severe punishment for his efforts. Yet in his heart he always reflected on the fact that he too was a foolish being, not better than those who opposed him. As he said in *Tannisho*:

> I know nothing at all of good or evil. For if I could know thoroughly, as Amida Buddha knows, that an act was good, then I would know good. If I could know thoroughly, as the Buddha knows, that an act was evil, then I would know evil. But with a foolish being full of blind passions, in this fleeting world—this burning house—all matters without exception are empty and false, totally without truth and sincerity. The nembutsu alone is true and real.

This is a remarkable statement for a revered Buddhist monk to make. Rather than claiming deep insight or profound understanding as most Buddhist leaders do, Shinran refuses to put himself above anyone else. When he speaks of the buddha alone understanding good and evil, he brings attention to the limits of our knowledge. None of us knows *thoroughly*, in the manner of a buddha. Buddhas see all the interconnections between all actions in the present and past; they see all the outcomes of every action, and understand human nature and the nature of each individual on a level that we unawakened people never access; they continually experience our inner togetherness. Thus, they can truly judge whether this or that action, this or that view, will lead to genuinely positive, negative, or mixed outcomes. (This is what good and evil are in Buddhism: not static moral positions, but judgments on the results of actions in consideration of whether they increase happiness or suffering in the world.) In this life, no one, not you nor I nor any Buddhist sage no matter how exalted, ever achieves this level of awareness.

Compared to a buddha, the gulf of "rightness" that I perceive between myself and my opponents shrinks to near imperceptibility. It's like a person standing on a chair next to a person standing on the ground: yes, the person on the chair is technically closer to the sun, but from the sun's point of view, is there really any difference? What a fool I would be if I crowed about my proximity to the sun from on top my chair! This is what it's like when I look down on those who disagree with me.

Shinran says that all matters are empty and false, truthless and insincere. What he's pointing out is our profound self-centredness in all things, our constant reference to ourselves in all situations and relationships. This self is the central problem in Buddhism; our misunderstanding of it and attachment to it rather than the fullness of our inter-relationality with others is the ultimate source of our suffering (and what causes us to bring suffering to others through our mis-actions). When I encounter the political and social realms, I do so from my limited perspective, and seek gains that will accrue to this foolish self. When I think of the natural world, I relate to it as something other than myself, something I enter, rather than something of which I am a part. Always my ego is pushing itself forward and seeking to maximize imagined gains and minimize imagined losses, even in my most charitable or seemingly selfless moments. This is true of other people as well, on both sides of every conflict.

Only the nembutsu is true and real. It is true and real because the nembutsu is not an act of self-gaining. Nembutsu, as taught by Shinran, is an expression of Great Compassion coming to us and moving through us. It enfolds the foolish self and all foolish selves, and gives voice to that inner togetherness which transcends selfishness. When we act to make the world better, we need to do so from a firm foundation of nembutsu, not self-centredness. Again and again in the midst of our work, we need to pause, say the nembutsu, and return to rest in the Primal Vow of Great Compassion for all beings.

Tannisho records a conversation between Shinran and his disciple Yuien-bo, the actual author/editor of the text. It is a key encounter that helps us to understand how to relate to ourselves and those we oppose:

> Shinran asked, "Yuien-bo, do you accept all that I say?"
>
> "Yes I do," I answered.
>
> "Then will you not deviate from whatever I tell you?" he repeated.
>
> I humbly affirmed this. Thereupon he said, "Now, I want you to kill a thousand people. If you do, you will definitely attain birth in the Pure Land."
>
> I responded, "Though you instruct me thus, I'm afraid it is not in my power to kill even one person."
>
> "Then why did you say that you would follow whatever I told you?" He continued, "By this you should realize that if we could always act as we wished, then when I told you to kill a thousand people in order to enter the Pure Land, you should have immediately done so. But since you lack the karmic cause inducing you to kill even a single person, you do not kill. It is not that you do not kill because your heart is good. In the same way, a person may not wish

> to harm anyone and yet end up killing a hundred or a thousand people."

Our differences with those whom we disagree with are not differences in kind—they are differences in circumstance. No person is inherently more moral or good or right than another. Were we born into another's situation, we might well make decisions very similar to them, decisions that seem strange or inexcusable to us in our momentarily current situations. I know this because my own ancestral past is full of people whose actions I abhor. My family tree includes pirates, kidnappers, slavers, land speculators, Confederates, bail bondsmen, Ku Klux Klan members, and countless others who robbed, abused, and harmed people, or acted as agents of systems of harm. These sorts of actions are in opposition to everything I believe in, to everything that I think of as core to what makes me myself. And yet, they are no different from me in any way whatsoever. They are my past and my DNA. That I do not enslave others or drive people off their ancestral land is not because I am somehow different from them—it is simply because of my profound good luck to be born in a time and place where I am not pushed toward such actions.

As a white North American of mainly British descent, there's a lot of particularly ugly stuff in my family's recent history. But this principle applies to all of us. Every single living person is descended from countless people who carried out unspeakable harms toward others and contributed to systems of oppression and exploitation, whether recently or somewhat further back in time. We differ from the worst of our past only in time and circumstance, not quality or nature. This is true of those we see on the "other side" of charged issues. No matter how angry we may feel toward our opponents, they are acting in ways that seem to make sense in their own situations, and were we in those situations with the conditioning they've experienced, we might act similarly. No matter how sure we are that our positions are the best for moving society forward and reducing suffering, we remain foolish beings, just like our opponents, with limited wisdom and poor ability to perceive our own motivations and feelings.

What Shinran's teachings point to is that the so-called evil and the foolish—whom we usually consider to be our opponents—are not our enemies. They are us. We too are evil and foolish in myriad ways. We must continually recognize our essential unity with those we think of as wrong or wicked. We must not pretend that we are pure saviors. We too are oppressors, caught in systems we dimly perceive, full of blindness and yet enabled to see in part due to the light of the Buddha. If we seek to act as bodhisattvas, we must be conscious of being *bombu* bodhisattvas, foolish bodhisattvas fumbling toward reunion with those who are temporarily on the other side.

This is more than just a necessary attitude for Jodo Shinshu engagement. It is also a guide for how to approach various issues. For example, Rennyo opposed the execution of prisoners, and the Minster's Association of the Buddhist Churches of America issued an official statement against capital punishment. This position makes sense in light of Shinran's teachings. A murderer causes terrible suffering, but their actions are not solely due to evil choices. Violence arises from the profound ignorance that we all share. It often erupts in circumstances or due to conditioning that might lead any of us to make the same mistake, even if we desperately wish to think of ourselves as peaceful people. To combat violent crime, the best approach is to remove the factors that often precipitate such circumstances: poverty, prejudice, oppression, hopelessness, addiction, access to firearms, and cultural scripts that encourage greed, dominance, or violent "solutions" to challenges in life. And if violence is committed, rehabilitation is the right answer.

An important example of this principle that I too am a foolish being is manifested in the Jodo Shinshu response to discrimination against Japanese outcastes (*burakumin*). Most of these oppressed people are members of Jodo Shinshu, both because it was one of the only traditions that accepted them and because it offered a path and practice that could be pursued from their place at the bottom of the feudal social hierarchy. However, this does not mean that the burakumin experience within Jodo Shinshu was perfect: discrimination against burakumin by Jodo Shinshu monks and institutions has a long, disgraceful history. In the 1920s the burakumin liberation movement rose to combat the injustices they suffered, including by Jodo Shinshu. Otani-ha (the second largest Jodo Shinshu group) was forced to confront how they had failed to live up to Shinran's nondiscriminatory approach to Buddhism. In many sessions between the 1920s and 1970s, Otani-ha official representatives listened to burakumin who confronted and denounced them, emotionally detailing the suffering that the sect had caused. These representatives bore witness to their role in burakumin oppression, admitted their faults, and accepted the blame they had earned by failing to live up to Shinran's teachings in their treatment of the oppressed. In doing so, they were saying that we too are foolish beings. Even those who profess to teach the all-embracing compassion of Amida Buddha fail and allow their ego and blind passions to drive them to acts in violation of the Dharma.

These encounters opened the eyes of Otani-ha. Audio tapes of the denunciation sessions are played to students during Jodo Shinshu monastic training, and topics of human rights and anti-oppression are required elements of monastic education. The struggle for equality by burakumin, women, and others is embedded as an ongoing concern via the sect's Department for the Promotion of Liberation Movements.

Our failures show that we are still essentially human, just as our opponents are. We must study the problems of the world and make our best effort at choosing the most compassionate, helpful actions to combat suffering. But in doing so we must never lose sight of our inner togetherness with those who act in ways we dislike, and our essential foolishness that is a universal component of human nature.

Fourth Principle
The Indebtedness of Interconnection

Buddhism's awareness of our interdependency with all things provides a beautiful and moving vision, one that spurs us to care for others because we see that they aren't really separate from ourselves. For Jodo Shinshu Buddhists specifically, there's a further level of meaning to our inner togetherness. The essence of the Pure Land teachings is often boiled down to a key phrase in the Jodo Shinshu tradition:

> *Shinjin shoin, shomyo ho-on*: "The trusting heart that we receive from Amida Buddha is the true cause of our liberation; we gratefully say the nembutsu as our response to the debt incurred by the Buddha's immeasurable years of effort in order to liberate us."

The heart of Jodo Shinshu Buddhism is relational: it is recognition of gifts received via hard work on our behalf, and response with gratitude to acknowledge and (partially) repay the debt that we've thus incurred. Having received, we have a responsibility to respond in kind. But Amida Buddha doesn't need anything from us—not worship, or donations, or pledges of loyalty, or anything else. This impasse is broken by saying the nembutsu, which "completes the circuit" between us and Amida Buddha, and by paying our debt forward to others who become the object of our efforts to express thanksgiving and compassion, as the buddha would wish us to do.

This centrality of relationality in Pure Land spirituality, and the basic formula of receipt-acknowledgement-indebtedness-action, drives Jodo Shinshu engagement. When we reflect on our situations, we see that our lives and awakening depend on constant receiving from others. With every breath we incur a debt to the air, the trees, the Earth. Countless factors are continually enabling us to live in every moment, to practice the Dharma, to experience love, happiness, and awakening. Even if we are vegan pacifists living off the grid, our living necessitates death for other organisms; and most of us are hardly model exemplars, no matter how much we may wish. Fossil fuels and other dirty energy sources underlie nearly every moment of comfort, convenience, or travel for most people; even the roads we drive our electric vehicles on are made by destructive polluting processes. Regardless of whatever our political beliefs may be, our taxes fund activities that are harmful and to which we would object. There is no way to stop incurring debt, for to live is to receive, until the very last moment.

This indebtedness is deep but shouldn't be depressing. It is the very nature of interdependence. If we weren't indebted, it would mean we were dead, or somehow had become so separated from everything else in the universe that we stood alone and isolated in a void of infinite loneliness. Being in debt is not shameful—it's the recognition that we receive and have an obligation to give, which is a wonderful and mature attitude.

It's recorded that Rennyo, one of the most important Jodo Shinshu leaders of the past, once saw a scrap of paper on the ground. He grabbed it and raised it to his head, exclaiming "How can you waste something that is given by the Buddha!" The combination of his impoverishment and his gratitude meant that he never wasted anything. He understood its value and that everything he received came to him through the efforts of others. As he put it, "What is there that is not the Buddha's gift?" This is rhetorical, of course: there is nothing whatsoever that is not Amida Buddha's gift. For as long as we live, we are receivers. For as long as we realize this truth, we should be givers.

This holds true in all situations, but it is especially clear in relation to the natural environment. We are an expression of this environment, and it is a fundamental wellspring for the existence of life. Yet our modern human activities pose serious threats to the health of our environment and the other beings who share it with us. Recognizing our indebtedness to the water, air, earth, beings, and processes that generate and support us, we should respond by trying to minimize harm and produce healing for the living world. We can see such appreciation and indebtedness in various eco-positive initiatives taken by Pure Land temples around the world and all others who join in this common cause.

Junkoin is a Pure Land temple in Japan, in the Jodo Shu tradition (a close cousin of Jodo Shinshu). They declared that awareness of the importance of the environment is central to their practice of Buddhism: "Human life as well as all life existing in nature is mutually interlinked and dependent on each other. This Buddhist concept aims at creating a global society of coexistence and co-prosperity. Junkoin, in solidarity not only with Buddhists but also with other citizens, NGOs, and various other groups, is dedicated to ecological development and human rights issues." To follow up on this sentiment, the temple was rebuilt with eco-friendly concrete and wood building materials, with designs intended to transform it into a green building that did not create waste or rely on polluting energy.

Among other features, the traditional ceramic roof tiles were replaced with large solar panels, as part of the effort to create a People's Power Plant. The purchase of the panels was funded by locals, who offered the solar tiles as a gift to the temple. Further donations were used to establish the Mirai ("Future") Bank at the temple, which gave out interest-free loans to locals so that they could buy environmentally-friendly refrigerators. The solar panels enabled the temple to cease its dependency on dirty energy sold by the city. Excess clean energy generated by the temple panels is sold cheaply to locals, enabling them to reduce their use of dirty energy, and there is so much that the temple is also able to sell it to the city at large, again cutting down the reliance on dirty energy. Similar concerns drive Tera Energy, an energy company created by Japanese Jodo Shinshu monks which stresses renewable energy, avoids nuclear-based energy, and donates a share of the user's bill to a positive initiative of their choice, such as building libraries and schools for ethnic minority children in various countries, regeneration of polluted areas, and sex education.

Junkoin also created a local currency for users of the People's Power Plant. It could be spent to buy babysitting, translation, and other services designed to deepen interpersonal relationships and trust in the community. The temple recognized that social disintegration and alienation from the sources that produce and support our living is part of what fuels the processes of environmental degradation (and human rights abuses, another grave concern for the temple). All these various actions—rebuilding, loaning, creating services—are models that our own local temples can contemplate implementing, for the betterment of our communities.

Fifth Principle
Action Expresses Gratitude

Our awareness of debt arises from our realization of the gifts we have received. This is a powerful motivator to check our actions to ensure they are in line with the Buddha's wish for an end to suffering. However, the most important aspect of Jodo Shinshu spirituality is gratitude. Shin Buddhism has been described as "the path of gratitude," which is an apt characterization. When practitioners of the path of sages make progress toward their goals, they can tell themselves that it is due to their vigorous efforts. But in Jodo Shinshu our spiritual awakening comes about through the working of power-beyond-self (*tariki*, which Rev. Hozen Seki explains "means *universal* or *natural* power"), and there is nothing we need do to bring it about. It is already accomplished by the Primal Vow that Dharmakara made in the timeless past. Our lot, as Jodo Shinshu Buddhists, is simply to respond with gratitude as we wake up to the compassion we receive. As Shinran said in *Tannisho*:

> The nembutsu that we say throughout our lives, thinking "If it weren't for this compassionate vow, how could such people as ourselves be liberated?" should be recognized as entirely the expression of our gratitude for the benevolence and our thankfulness for the working of Amida's great compassion.

Nembutsu doesn't do anything other than express our thankfulness. It isn't a prayer or petition; it doesn't generate merit or cause awakening. It is the response to our initial awakening, which comes about by receiving the fruits of the merit accumulated on our behalf by Amida Buddha: the trusting heart, which leads us to the Pure Land, where awakening is completed.

Shinran affirms in *A Collection of Letters* that the first nembutsu we say upon being awakened is a pure expression of joy. Thereafter, he counsels, the further nembutsu that we say should be directed toward the sentient beings who share this world with us, as a way of responding to the benevolence of Shakyamuni Buddha and Amida Buddha.

Realization of receiving benefits and the arising of gratitude lead to action. This is the natural way: as we feel thankful, we seek to respond. The formal expression of this thankfulness is spoken nembutsu, the sigh of relief and cry of joy that spills from us as Great Compassion lifts the load from our shoulders and illuminates our lives. The everyday, informal expression of this thankfulness takes the form of acts of kindness and charity. Rev. Hozen Seki gave an example of this from his early ministry, when he established the Jodo Shinshu temple in Phoenix. There were about a dozen feral cats and kittens that roamed the grounds of the temple. They followed Mrs. Seki around, and she fed them and talked to them kindly. But Rev. Seki was indifferent to them, and they would scatter whenever he came outside. They could sense a non-cat-lover. Then, as Rev. Seki narrated:

> One early September morning I received a telephone call from the hospital, where my wife had been admitted the night before. She had given birth to a baby boy, and both mother and son were fine. I burst with joy. Immediately, without thinking, I went to the icebox and took out all the food and brought it to the cats. What a surprised look they had! I still remember their faces as they cautiously ate the food. True, heartfelt happiness automatically reflects outwardly.

The act of giving food to the temple cats was nembutsu in that moment: action performed out of grateful happiness. Activism to help reduce the suffering of the world can also be carried out as nembutsu. When performed from the grateful heart, social and political action are a type of nembutsu too. They gladden the heart of Amida Buddha, who wishes all beings to be freed from pain and misery.

In other forms of Buddhism, positive action in the world accumulates merit, and is part of the path to sainthood. But action performed as grateful nembutsu doesn't take us closer to becoming saints. It isn't going to take us to buddhahood. It can be deeply spiritually rewarding, but it is not done in pursuit of rewards: it is undertaken out of recognition that we have already received so much, and our feelings of thankfulness need to be channeled into expression.

An example of action undertaken out of a feeling of gratitude and wish to extend what one has received to others is Project Dana, a major initiative started by two Jodo Shinshu women, Shimeji Kanazawa and Rose Nakamura, at the Mo'ili'ili Hongwanji Jodo Shinshu temple in Honolulu. Still based at the Jodo Shinshu temple but very much inter-faith in spirit, Project Dana today includes dozens of temples and churches with over 1000 volunteers. They provide support that allows housebound elders to live in dignity and independence, as an expression of the Buddhist value of *dana* (selfless giving). Project Dana provides in-person and phone visitations to isolated seniors, home repair, home safety assessments, decluttering, assistance in medical equipment set-up, and transportation to medical appointments, grocery shopping, religious services, banking, and government offices. Crucially, Project Dana also provides support to caregivers. They train them, host caregiver support groups, provide one-on-one counseling, and celebrate them with quarterly outings. Embodying the Pure Land vision of universal embrace, they nurture both caregivers and receivers.

Sixth Principle
Circulation of Compassion

Tannisho states that "Becoming one with the unhindered light filling the universe, we will benefit all sentient beings." This statement is made in reference to the Pure Land, and raises a point of vital importance. Because of the influence of Christianity in the West, it is easy to mistakenly imagine that the Pure Land is simply a Buddhist analog of Heaven, a place of eternal rest and peace as a reward for faithfulness. Nothing could be further from the truth.

Birth in the Pure Land is the true beginning of our spiritual work, not the end. In Shinran's understanding, those who are born in the Pure Land instantly become one with true reality, and immediately return to this world to work at relieving the suffering of those still trapped in ignorance and woe. In accord with

Dharmakara's twenty-second vow in the *Larger Pure Land Sutra*, the beings of the Pure Land act as great bodhisattvas speeding from the Pure Land to beings throughout the universe to liberate them. As Shinran says in *Tannisho*, "Compassion in the Pure Land path should be understood as first attaining buddhahood quickly through saying the nembutsu and, with the mind of great love and compassion, freely benefiting sentient beings as one wishes." Attaining buddhahood is actually the easy part, enabled by the skillful means of the Pure Land developed by Amida Buddha. Next, we roll up our sleeves to spread the mind of great love and compassion to others, acting on our deepest wish that all beings be sprung from the prison of suffering.

Empowered by the Great Compassion, bodhisattvas constantly circulate to and from the Pure Land, the state of nirvana, ceaselessly working to help others stuck in the world of birth-and-death. In this way the Pure Land and our everyday reality are intimately connected, not separated from each other. For the bodhisattvas, they are simply two sides of experience: life experienced in its ultimate liberated state, and life experienced from within the ego shell of ignorant foolishness.

The Pure Land is reality in its truest state. It is something that we never fully achieve while stuck in this world of karmic entanglement, but we do experience it in a limited fashion through the power of the trusting heart, and, with the sangha of the Pure Land as our model, we work to make our imperfect society and environment better. It's a never-ending task—the perfect Pure Land cannot be built on Earth—but we can move in the right direction together. The bodhisattvas are constantly helping us to build it and they show us the active spirit that directs us on the right path.

To constantly circulate compassion is to keep going when it seems like no progress is being made, or even when things seem to be getting worse. It means to keep coming back to the same problems over and over, never abandoning anyone to languish in suffering. Even if we need to sometimes pause and recharge with a reconnection to the Pure Land, inevitably we return to keep working for others so long as suffering exists. It seems like a tall order, but there are two important facets of constantly circulating compassion that need to be noted. First is the ability to reconnect with the Pure Land through the nembutsu, so that we let the parts of ourselves that wear down be buoyed by the always-embracing power of Great Compassion. Second is the nature of constant circulation: it is not an individual task. Bodhisattvas don't heal the world by themselves. They do it as part of the Sangha of Boundless Life, the fellowship of awakening beings that find solidarity in the inner togetherness revealed by the Dharma.

Among the various flavours of Pure Land practice in Japan, one important strain was Yuzu Nembutsu. This tradition taught that nembutsu is fractal in nature: one nembutsu echoes throughout the universe to heal all beings, and all nembutsu pronounced by others, wherever they may be, reaches and supports the awakening of yourself. You are not an isolated individual chanting in a sea of strangers—your nembutsu embraces everyone, and the nembutsu that we utter soothes and empowers you on levels beyond ordinary consciousness. We never practice or struggle alone.

An example of how bodhisattvas of the Pure Land act is found in Jodo Shinshu activism around nuclear energy in Japan. On March 11, 2011, there was a terrible triple disaster: an earthquake caused a tsunami, which caused nuclear pollution to leak from the damaged Fukushima power plant. The following year, grassroots Jodo Shinshu communities feared that the ongoing suffering of those in the affected areas, and the threat of repeated disasters due to the presence of nuclear plants elsewhere in Japan, was being gradually swept under the table by the government. In response, they organized a day of protest, including a service, lectures, and a march to Shinran's grave while holding banners with the nembutsu and slogans demanding action. As the issue has faded, they've repeatedly worked to bring the suffering of Fukushima back into people's minds, so that the affected can continue to receive the aid they need. They support one another in this endeavor: it isn't the work of heroic solo activists; it is community effort that circulates the necessary compassion among each other. Together they move forward to help those in need.

In conclusion, Jodo Shinshu spiritual principles have personal and social applications. This is hardly surprising, given that Jodo

Shinshu was born as a people's Buddhism and has dramatically affected the course of Japanese society at multiple points in history. Working for the benefit of others is an application of our principles and values, and this work deepens our understanding and connection to the Dharma. In the spirit of Shinran and in harmony with the Primal Vow of Amida Buddha, we can find guidance in the teachings for how to help heal our suffering world.

6

Concepts for Engaged Shin Buddhism

In this final chapter I want to explore some concepts related to the Pure Land way which may help us understand how to apply the engaged Jodo Shinshu principles found in the previous chapter. Pure Land as a way of emancipation holds great potential for us to help society and the Earth, and in the process, we may come to better understand the deepest meaning of Amida Buddha's Primal Vow and how it operates to liberate us from blind passions. These concepts can help establish some basic vocabulary for those who are newer to Pure Land Buddhism, point us to deeper understandings for those who are already familiar with the Pure Land way, and provide common language for dialogue with other Buddhist lineages and interfaith activists.

Great Compassion

As Pure Land Buddhists, we entrust ourselves to Great Compassion. This Great Compassion can be described as a quality or characteristic of Amida Buddha; as well, we can simply say that Amida Buddha is Great Compassion. Great Compassion is what we call the *Dharmakaya*, the true nature of things. Because it can't be directly understood by us ordinary beings, it is given the form of Amida Buddha so that we can have something to which to relate. This is the key: Amida Buddha, Great Compassion, Dharmakaya—these are things to which we relate, rather than fully understand. Jodo Shinshu is a Buddhism based more on feeling than on thoughts, with the heart as a path to awakening rather than a cerebral intellectual path based on the mind. This doesn't mean that the mind is neglected, only that we prioritize attitudes and feelings over abstract ideas. Rev. Hozen Seki expresses this feeling of awakening to truth through relationship with Great Compassion:

> The voice of the Buddha will not leave me. I am living within this Great Compassion. Heaven and Earth and everything without exception will settle in Amida Buddha's Compassion. The sound of the wind and the sound of the waves are none other than the voice of the Nembutsu.
>
> We are born in Nembutsu, raised in Nembutsu, and die in Nembutsu, becoming Amida Butsu. Let us rejoice to have been able to be received by Nembutsu. Our meeting with Nembutsu is the key to peaceful living, and this is the Great Natural Way. I can only say "Thank you," reciting *Namu Amida Butsu.*

One of my friends and mentors in Japan is Tatsuguchi Myosei, a retired professor of Buddhist Studies at Ryukoku University and a Jodo Shinshu monk from a long line of family priests. For me, he exemplifies Great Compassion in its teaching, supportive aspect. Since we both enjoy visiting historic temples, we've traveled together to scores of places in Kyoto, Osaka, Hiroshima, and elsewhere. When you spend so much time on trains with someone, you end up learning a lot, and that's been true of my relationship with Dr. Tatsuguchi.

One time we were on the train headed to a temple in Nara, and I was reading a famous collection of sayings by and about Rennyo, the 15th century Jodo Shinshu leader. I remarked to Dr. Tatsuguchi about a passage concerning what sort of images Rennyo felt we should enshrine on our altars. Rennyo said that a statue of Amida Buddha is OK, but that a painting of Amida is better. And even better than a painting would be a simple calligraphy reading "Namo Amida Butsu." The reason is that when we have a physical statue, it's easy to make the mistake of thinking of Amida as a solid, human-looking person whom we might meet walking down the street someday. The same mistake can be made by looking at a painting, though at least it's less three dimensional. But the nembutsu is abstract and therefore points us on to the reality of Amida Buddha as the light of boundless wisdom and compassion, which is how Shinran thought about Amida.

When I read this passage to Dr. Tatsuguchi, he nodded in agreement with Rennyo. But after a moment he commented, "Nothing at all is best." I thought that was a very good statement. No image at all. This would prevent us from turning Amida into some sort of idol. Ultimately, the image of Amida is intended as a skillful means that points us on toward true reality, which, as Shinran explained, is beyond form or colour.

But if we have no image, it's easy to feel like we're abandoned or have nothing to take refuge in. This world is difficult, and even if reality as the Buddhas understand it is beyond form or concepts, we are still ordinary beings and need such things to help us out. That is why I was grateful that Dr. Tatsuguchi didn't stop there. After he said "Nothing at all is best," he paused for a moment, and then put his hands together in gassho. "Or maybe it would be best to do this," he said, and bowed in gassho in several directions. To me, this was a very deep understanding. He didn't go beyond form and then just leave me high and dry, with nothing to bow toward. Instead, he went beyond form and concepts by bowing toward all directions and all things as indicating the presence of Great Compassion. Amida isn't contained in a statue, or in a painting, or even in a calligraphy of the name. Great Compassion is always everywhere, supporting us and working to wake us up. Wherever we look, whether at the beautiful statue in the temple or the leaves moving in the breeze, we can see it and feel grateful.

This Great Compassion is the Jodo Shinshu understanding of buddha-nature. As Shinran quotes in the *Kyogyoshinsho*, "Great Love and Great Compassion are called buddha-nature. Why? Because Great Love and Great Compassion always accompany the bodhisattva, just as shadows accompany things. All sentient beings will without fail ultimately realize Great Love and Great Compassion. Therefore, it is taught, 'All sentient beings are possessed of buddha-nature.' Great Love and Great Compassion are buddha-nature. Buddha-nature is Tathagata."

Elsewhere Shinran explains that this Great Compassion is realizing true reality, attaining emancipation. "When persons attain this enlightenment," he says, "with Great Love and Great Compassion immediately reaching their fullness in them, they return to the ocean of birth-and-death to save all sentient beings." Great Compassion is the completion of the Buddhist way, the fulfilment/realization of buddha-nature, and it spurs the awakened heart to plunge into the suffering world on behalf of those yet to be emancipated.

Great Compassion is what embraces us and enables our liberation. It doesn't judge, demand, or request anything of us to become worthy to receive help. Great Compassion just helps, period. It is non-discriminating (however, it does prefer to first help those who suffer the most, as they are in the greatest need). Great Compassion is all-embracing and takes on any form that helps. Thus, Great Compassion comes to us in the form of Namo Amida Butsu, and also in the form of those who teach the Dharma, those who give aid to the suffering, those who stand up for the marginalized, and many other wondrous forms.

Shinran approvingly quotes the Pure Land master Genshin in the *Kyogyoshinsho*: "[Amida] Buddha's regard for each sentient being with eyes of compassion is equal, as though each one was the buddha's only child; hence, I take refuge in and worship the unsurpassed mother of great compassion." Great Compassion is not only what we receive, but also what we become through the Pure Land way, as Shinran states in a hymn:

When a person realizes the mind of non-discrimination,
that attainment is the
"state of regarding each being as one's only child."
This is none other than buddha-nature;
We will awaken to it on reaching the land of peace.

The final realization of Great Compassion comes only upon total immersion in the Pure Land, a situation that is impossible while we struggle with karmic entanglements in our lives. But though we can't yet fully embody Amida Buddha's non-discrimination, it provides the guiding star for our conduct. With gratitude, we try to emulate Great Compassion, to become a vehicle for Great Compassion's working in this suffering world. And the more we turn toward others as if they were our own kin, the more we discover that Great Compassion is reaching toward us.

Going/Returning

To understand how Pure Land practice can lead to social action to reduce suffering, it helps to recognize the active nature of the Jodo Shinshu path. Because we focus on receiving wisdom from beyond the self, it's possible to mistake Pure Land Buddhism as passive and inert. But that would restrict our field of vision too narrowly. When we cast our gaze forwards and backwards in time, we discover the highly active function of Great Compassion propelling us along the bodhisattva path. This is encapsulated in the Jodo Shinshu doctrine of *oso eko/genso eko*: receiving the merit to go toward awakening and receiving the merit to return and share the liberation that one has received.

Going and returning is the fundamental activity of the Pure Land practitioner. We're enabled to go to the Pure Land by Great Compassion and enabled to return from the Pure Land by Great Compassion, to assist those trapped in suffering. We go initially during this lifetime and return initially during this lifetime. Our initial going is not complete, just as our ability to return and truly help is only partial. But it is a real awakening, and through it we can express Great Compassion, even though the final release from our karmic entanglements occurs at the end of life.

Rev. Kenryu Tsuji was the first North American-born bishop of the Buddhist Churches of America. Raised on a farm in British Columbia, he had a deep sense of how the natural rhythms of life mirror the activities of Great Compassion's working in our lives. As he explained it once,

> Death is neither the end of life nor the termination of life's activity. Waters of the river flow onward to reach the wide expanse of the sea. In time, the water evaporates and becomes clouds.

When moisture saturates cumulus clouds it is released, returning to the surface of the earth as rain. From the skies the rain sustains the life of all living things, from the tallest redwoods to the tiniest crawling insects.

Water flowing in the sea may be called oso eko, the going phase of movement. Raindrops falling to the earth may be seen as genso eko, that is, water returning to its place of origin.

Shinran, just before he died, said "When my life has run its course, I shall go to the Pure Land and return again, like waves of the Wako-no-Ura bay breaking upon the shore.... When two of you rejoice, remember there are three, as Shinran will be there too."

All human life is a source of energy, of compassion stored in the depth of its innate buddhahood. It may be only a microscopic part of the cosmic compassion of the universe, which we religiously call Amida Buddha.

But once immersed in the cosmic compassion, this energy is a mighty current flowing harmoniously. Human beings are so attached to the body that it is thought that death of the body is the end of everything. In reality, it is the beginning of interaction with the entire universe.

When the body is buried in the ground, it becomes soil in which all living things grow. Shinran Shonin said, "When I die, throw my body in the Kamo river to feed the fish." He was realizing oneness with all forms of life.

As the body is cremated, smoke rises heavenward and gas molecules enter the atmosphere that we breathe. This is the influence of physical energy. Human life is more than just physical energy. It is also moral and spiritual energy released upon the whole world.

Intangible influence is often difficult to perceive.

> Nonetheless, it continues to function throughout the universe. How many times have we read the words of Buddha and other masters for inspiration, comfort, strength, and a practical guide to living?
>
> How many times have you picked up an old letter written by your long-departed mother or father, wife or husband, and quietly contemplated its contents?
>
> Just as waters of the river return from the ocean to quench a thirsty planet, human energy now purified in buddhahood—the Pure Land—returns to the world, continuing its perpetual work of compassion. This is genso eko [the returning phase].
>
> Too often the Pure Land is considered a static place of eternal rest far removed from the affairs of worldly beings. Contrary to this belief, the true Pure Land is where cosmic compassion is generated and perpetually regenerated.

As Rev. Tsuji explained, the Jodo Shinshu way of awakening by going and sharing awakening by returning is a natural process, like that of water. Floating on the Primal Vow, we are taken to the headwaters of awakening and enabled to flow back downstream to nurture others. As we pursue an end to suffering in this world through kindness, charity, and action, we continually immerse ourselves in (go to) the Pure Land and work to spread relief from suffering (return).

Rev. Seki put it this way (pardon the archaic gendered language, by the way—Amida Buddha is beyond gender): "The important thing, then, is *to become an awakened one.* Awakening is to become Amida Buddha himself. And if there is one single being who cannot awaken, Amida himself will not awaken. When we awaken, Amida Buddha's vow and action become our vow and action. Not dwelling in any paradise, we work continuously for the salvation of others. This teaching is always action upon action, marching and marching, for the sake of all sentient beings. There is no rest." In other words, the Pure Land way is an active way, because we are moved to do something about the suffering of others. As Amida

Buddha's vow becomes our own vow, the Buddha's helping action becomes our own: we work in the world so that Great Compassion can flow through us and on to all beings.

Sangha of Boundless Life

The Pure Land way is the path of sangha. In our tradition sangha means community, and it is within, through, and with the community that we progress toward awakening. This contrasts with more individualistic forms of Buddhism, which concentrate on heroic solo practices or one's own accumulation of merit. For us, practice is always communal and relational: with Amida Buddha, with the local community of practitioners, and with all sentient beings. It is from the Buddha that we receive awakening; it is with the community that we achieve awakening; it is for all beings that we share awakening.

Jodo Shinshu philosopher Nobuo Haneda made a very important point:

> No matter how capable a seed may be, it cannot sprout by itself. If a seed is placed on a rock, it will never sprout. It must have conditions such as heat, moisture, and light. The Pure Land (the Sangha) is the condition that enables us to sprout. It is by receiving power from the Pure Land, from the Sangha, that we can sprout and eventually bear fruit.
>
> Realistically speaking, among the Three Treasures (i.e., the Buddha, the Dharma, and the Sangha), the Sangha is the most important. Becoming a member of the Sangha, of a living tradition, is the most important thing in Buddhism. It is the Sangha that enables us to gain insight into the Buddha and the Dharma. Thus, Shin Buddhism says that birth in the Pure Land (the Sangha) is the most important thing. Our birth in the Pure Land, our becoming part of the Sangha, is our liberation.

When we are born in the Pure Land, we are born into the sangha of Amida Buddha. The name "Amida" literally means "Boundless"—it is a contraction of one of the Buddha's original Sanskrit names, "Boundless Life." This Boundless Life exists endlessly to help liberate all beings. Because it is boundless, it includes us and all forms of life: if our lives are not included, then there would be a boundary, an exclusion zone.

Our participation in the sangha of Boundless Life occurs in three stages. First, all living things are included in the sangha of Boundless Life, without exception. Since beginningless time, this Boundless Life has been embracing us. However, we are usually ignorant of how Great Compassion is working upon us, and we cling to ourselves while seeing others as problems.

Second, when the trusting heart awakens within us, we join the ranks of those who know they are part of the sangha of Boundless Life. Our load becomes lighter, our hearts become freer, and gratitude wells up, gushing forth as nembutsu. As our lives continue, we soak in the Dharma and seek to spread happiness and release from suffering to others.

Third, when we die, the tight knot of elements that we clung to as our "selves" unravels and submerges completely in the reality of Boundless Life. From there we return as Namo Amida Butsu, as wind, as light, as birdsong, as any form necessary to help those who still need to awaken and be freed from pain and stress. The Pure Land teacher Ippen put it well: "Among all living things—mountains and rivers, grasses and trees, even the sounds of blowing winds and rising waves—there is nothing that is not the nembutsu. It is not human beings alone who share in the all-surpassing Vow."

One thing that the Pure Land sutras teach is that there is not a separation of people from the surrounding environment. The beings of the Pure Land are part of its adornments, just as the trees and pools are. They aren't visitors to a space that is fundamentally other than what they are. They are part of it, part of its charms and wonders. On Earth, the same is true. We shouldn't say that there are humans *and* the natural environment. We are not interlopers, visitors, or trespassers. We are of the Earth and there is no land environment where we have not always been for many thousands of years. The idea of pristine Nature is a myth, born mainly of colonial arrogance and urban romanticism: there has never been an unpopulated, undiscovered country where there are only animals, plants, and pure water and sky, where we can go to escape the din of industrial cities. Every inch of the so-called New World was walked by Indigenous people who altered it by their presence for generations beyond counting: cultivating gardens and forests; hunting animals whose shifting behaviours changed the course of streams; practicing controlled burns that renewed forests and prevented disastrous wildfires; and so on. So too in Europe, Africa, and everywhere. In the North, Inuit and other Indigenous people roamed as far as life could be sustained; surely even Antarctic waters and perhaps the continent were visited by hunters and explorers following the fish and whales. Only the deep seas have ever been unwalked by humans, and even there they were hardly unconnected to us in the interdependent web of life.

We must not think of ourselves as monsters or cancers doing grievous harm to an innocent Nature. That mentality is wrong. It already separates us from Nature, which is the source of the problem in the first place. We are of Nature and will always have the right to be here. Earth is sick without us. We are part of it and should remain. But we need to stop making our Earth sick by our behaviour. We need to adjust our thinking and ways of living so that we fit better with the other living things around us, acknowledging that we are just one part of the sangha of Boundless Life. In the Pure Land, the beings and the trees, birds, and pools all exist in absolute harmony, and that is why it is pure and beautiful. We need to return to harmony, for the health of ourselves, the trees, birds, and waters of this Earth of which we are a part. A good example of this awareness is found in Winnipeg, where the local Jodo Shinshu Buddhists inducted an elm tree outside the temple as a member of the congregation.

Environmental concerns have been part of the Jodo Shinshu temples in North America for decades. One of the recent manifestations is the EcoSangha movement within the Buddhist Churches of America. EcoSangha recognizes our role as members of the sangha of Boundless Life and the responsibility this entails. Local chapters work to educate their temple about how to follow sustainable practices, and host events exploring the intersection of Buddhism and ecology.

The BCA's EcoSangha movement was founded by Jodo Shinshu minister Rev. Donald Castro, with important organizational support from lay leader Karen Akahoshi. As part of his Buddhist ecological ministry, Rev. Castro teaches a unique form of *naikan*. Naikan is a Japanese psychotherapy, derived from Jodo Shinshu Buddhism. In EcoSangha naikan, the practitioner is encouraged to ask themselves three questions every day and reflect on the answers: What have I done today *for* Mother Earth? What have I done today *to* Mother Earth? What has Mother Earth done today for *me*? From this comes deepened awareness and commitment. We can extend this to the level of the sangha, so that the temple reflects: what have we done for Mother Earth? What have we done today to Mother Earth? What has Mother Earth done for us today? This stimulates a desire to make the practices of the sangha as ecologically sustainable as possible, and to make the temple as positive a presence in the land as possible. Naturally this leads on to the wider community level, where we as citizens ask what we have done for, done to, and received from Mother Earth, and thus with awareness and gratitude work to reshape society's impact on and relationship to our environment.

Rev. Castro places particular emphasis on the classic image of the seated Buddha reaching down to touch the earth with his hand. When the Buddha touches the Earth, it speaks and says he has a right to be here, on the seat of enlightenment. It is a moment of mutual recognition: the Buddha recognizes that the Earth has been his partner in awakening, and the Earth recognizes that the Buddha has struggled against his greed and ignorance to reach a point of genuine understanding and compassion. It is Buddha and Earth seeing each other, after a long journey of awakening together. Nor is it the only or first touch. Even before the Buddha extends his hand, he is touching the Earth with his legs and body. He is touching the Earth's air with his skin and hair. He is touching it constantly because it is constantly supporting him. But perhaps until that hand reaches out, he is not fully *in touch* with the Earth and the interdependent web that supports and nurtures his life and awakening. It is only at the moment which leads to buddhahood that he discovers the depth of his debt and interwovenness, and reaches out in kinship to all that supports him. This gesture is undertaken by all bodhisattvas as they near awakening. Dharmakara Bodhisattva too, in the process of becoming Boundless Life, touched the Earth and was affirmed by it.

The Environmental Teachers of the Pure Land

According to the sutras, the Pure Land is filled with music. It's basically a non-stop concert or rave, as music fills the air. Not only are there musicians, but the wind in the trees also makes delightful music. And then there are the birds. As the *Smaller Pure Land Sutra* describes:

> In the Pure Land there are always many kinds of rare and beautiful birds of various colours, such as swans, peacocks, parrots, mynah birds, kalavinkas, and jivamjivakas [gumyochos]. Six times a day birds sing with melodious and delicate sounds, which proclaim such teachings as the five roots of goodness, the five powers, the seven practices leading to Enlightenment, and the Noble Eightfold Path. On hearing them, all the people of that land are mindful of the Buddha, the Dharma, and the Sangha.... These birds are manifested by Amida so that their singing can proclaim and spread the Dharma.

So, there are six types of birds that are named as species that live in the Pure Land. And they are more than just animals: they are themselves teachers, who demonstrate the Dharma to us.

The last bird on the list is the gumyocho, which is not an ordinary species. We can see carvings of it on the altar tables placed before the statue of Amida Buddha in Jodo Shinshu temples. It's unmistakable: it has two heads. This is part of its teaching function. There's a famous story about this bird. The two heads had their own personalities and, being self-centred like all of us, they often quarreled. One head became extremely angry at the other, seeing it as an enemy. So it gave some poisoned food to the other head to kill it. Of course, since they shared a single body, they both died. As the first head was dying, it realized the utter foolishness of its actions and was awakened, and Amida Buddha placed the bird in the Pure Land so that it could teach its insight to others. The meaning of this story is pretty clear: it illustrates the Buddhist principle that we are all connected and that what hurts another person also hurts ourselves.

Another bird that is mentioned in the sutra is the peacock. This shouldn't surprise us, as peacocks are widely viewed as one of the most beautiful kinds of birds. But there's a further significance to peacocks for Pure Land Buddhism. Not only are they birds of the Pure Land, but it's also said that Amida Buddha rides on a peacock as his personal mount.

We don't depict Amida that way in the Jodo Shinshu tradition, but it's common in the art of some other forms of Buddhism. The reason we don't use this image is because Jodo Shinshu is very strict about proper Buddha images in temples. We only use a standing Amida Buddha, leaning slightly forward. There is a genuine purpose behind this. Sitting buddhas, whether on a lotus or an animal or whatever, are relatively passive. But in Jodo Shinshu images, Amida is standing up, springing into action to help others, and even leans forward as the Buddha comes rushing to liberate us all. We don't have to go to Amida and beg for entrance into the Pure Land, like in other forms of Buddhism. We understand that Great Compassion comes to us, just as we are, entering our ordinary foolish stressed-out lives to provide comfort and relief from suffering.

That's an important point. But it's still interesting that some other Buddhists prefer to depict Amida Buddha riding on a peacock. Why is there such an association of peacocks with Amida and the Pure Land?

In the wild in Asia, peacocks are fierce enemies of snakes. They won't allow snakes to live in their territories, and when they encounter a poisonous snake such as a cobra, they kill and eat it. This is why peacocks are significant: they signify the Buddhist principle of transforming poison into medicine. The peacock encounters a deadly snake, but instead of being defeated by it, the peacock consumes the snake and is not affected by its poison. Using the snake as nourishment, its body is strengthened and it is able to grow beautiful feathers. The incredible plumage of a peacock is a product of the poison that it ingested and transformed.

This is a Buddhist idea because it illustrates how the Dharma works. The Buddha points out that we suffer, and suffering poisons our lives. But by learning how suffering works and immersing ourselves in the Dharma, our suffering becomes the cause for our awakening and liberation. Thus, the poison of suffering is used as the medicine to relieve suffering.

Life provides us with many opportunities to turn poison into medicine, which is to say, to turn bad circumstances into something positive. For example, the height of the COVID-19 pandemic was a terrible experience for most of us. Many people died, many more got sick, and we suffered from job loss, disconnection from our friends and relatives, and all sorts of difficult disruptions to our normal lives. The coronavirus has certainly been a poison for us.

But at the same time, the pandemic lockdowns also presented us with opportunities. In the past, our temples never had the capacity to create online Dharma services, and we were isolated to listening to the same speaker each week, or spending a lot of money to fly in occasional guest speakers. But during the pandemic we managed to coordinate an online service with all the Jodo Shinshu ministers of Canada chanting together as one. We learned from guest speakers across the world on our screens and found ways to recreate some sangha-feeling in the virtual world. People who couldn't come to in-person services due to disability, age, or geography were enabled to hear the Dharma. All of this was only possible because we came together and were determined to eke some medicine out of the poison of our times. The hard times of the pandemic were the stimulus for creativity and solidarity.

This doesn't mean that the suffering of the pandemic was worth it. The point is that suffering is always going to happen, whether there is a pandemic or not. That's the First Noble Truth, that there is suffering in life. When suffering occurs, when something poisons our lives, we can take it as an opportunity to try to produce something good out of the situation.

My uncle died (of cancer) during this time. He was a role model for me for many years, and he was a very important part of the family. Even though it wasn't unexpected, I was very saddened about the loss, and the impact it had on my aunt, my parents, and my cousins. Because of the pandemic, I couldn't spend time with him before he died. And I couldn't attend his funeral, unlike the rest of my family, since they all live in the United States. I didn't get to say goodbye or to comfort my family in a meaningful way.

But his death was also the opportunity to transform poison into medicine. My uncle was an important scientist, and his death brought the scientific community together to celebrate his contributions and see how they could make sure his work continues. I couldn't be there myself, but the rest of my family gathered together in a way that they hadn't for many years, and his funeral became a chance to renew family bonds and make plans for future gatherings. My dad and my aunt told stories about my uncle when he was young that many people hadn't heard before, so the newer generations learned more about their heritage and the man who helped shape their lives.

This process is part of why funerals and memorials are stressed as important moments in Jodo Shinshu. Because everyone is embraced by Great Compassion and liberated through the Pure Land, we have no fear for our loved ones' fates and there is no need for a ritual to try and alter their afterlife. Rather, Jodo Shinshu memorials are an occasion for remembering the love of one who has returned to the Pure Land, for strengthening our bonds with those who are still living, and for reconnecting again with the message of Buddhism. Through funerals and memorials, we experience mourning with the sangha and listen to the words of the Dharma—this is how we work to transform the poison of loss into the medicine of comfort and insight.

We can take inspiration from the teachings of the birds of the Pure Land and turn it into concrete action. For instance, we've all noticed how poisonous the online environment is. People routinely treat each other like dirt, calling them all sorts of names, harassing them, because they can do it from the safety of their computer or phone, without having to deal with the consequences of hurting someone. This is especially true on social media, like Twitter and Facebook. It's a big problem, especially for women, people of colour, LGBTQ+ persons, and people concerned with politics and society.

I started a small-scale response to this poisonous online pattern. I call it the Peacock Project. When I see someone post a comment that attacks someone for their gender, race, or sexuality, I always leave a comment that supports the original person and affirms their humanity. I use the poisonous comment as a stimulus to provide a positive reply.

In my line of work, as a university professor, we're increasingly under attack from right-wing groups that don't want us to teach about the history of race and gender in North America. It's worse in the United States, but we see it here in Canada too, especially in relation to teaching about the true history of Canadian treatment of Indigenous peoples. Professors also get attacked for teaching about climate change and other scientific matters. There is an entire industry of media designed to provoke outrage and then direct it in mass online attacks against historians and scientists.

When I see this happening to a colleague, I activate the Peacock Project. I donate money to a charity of their choice, and petition my other colleagues to do the same. So, for instance when a colleague at a university in Florida was targeted because she posted some facts about LGBTQ+ people's negative experiences with some Buddhist groups, I sent around a request and we donated enough money to send a transgender child to summer camp. I call it the Peacock Project because we turn poison into medicine by responding to negativity with a positive outcome.

For me, this is a way to practice the compassion that Amida Buddha models for us. Transforming poison into medicine is the fundamental activity of Amida Buddha. Although none of us can transform our poisons as truly as Amida Buddha does, hopefully we can take this principle with us and do what we can to turn bad situations toward some good, and to find potential for awakening in moments of suffering and loss. That's what we do during the age of DharmaFail: things are falling apart, but we can sometimes take their very brokenness as an opportunity to spread compassion. When someone is attacked, we respond by healing them *and* the world: we support them in their suffering, and we contribute to the community on their behalf. The compassion is circulated, and a network of support is developed.

Beyond the music and birds, another of the adornments of the Pure Land are the dazzling flowers and refreshing waters. One of the favourite lines from the *Smaller Pure Land Sutra*, which ministers love to quote in their Dharma talks, is this description of the flowers of the Pure Land:

> In the ponds are lotuses as large as chariot-wheels—
> the blue ones radiating a blue light,
> the yellow a yellow light, the red a red light,
> and the white a white light.
> They are all marvelous
> and beautiful, fragrant and pure.

As with all things in the Pure Land, this isn't just a nice description of a lovely place. The Pure Land is not a vacation spot: it is a form of teaching, and all aspects of the Pure Land are illustrations of important Dharma lessons.

The flowers of the Pure Land are accepted and valued just as they are. The lotuses have different colours, but each one is marvelous, beautiful, and pure just as it is. No matter what colour they are, that colour shines out from them to beautify the world. For Jodo Shinshu Buddhists, this is a teaching about us. Whatever colour we are, whomever we are, we are all beautiful, we are all accepted, we all shine.

No colour is superior to any other. Thus, no race or ethnicity is superior to any other. All flowers are equal to each other. Therefore, all genders, sexualities, and types of people are equal to one another. All add value and wonder to our world. No light outshines any other: all shine in harmony in the waters of the Pure Land. They are all beautiful just as they are, and are all beautiful with one another. This is the vision of the Pure Land, the vision we are enjoined to bring to our everyday interactions with all the beautiful different people of our world.

Bombuness

In most forms of Buddhism, the practice is to strive at becoming a sage: someone unusually wise, morally superior, and exceptionally compassionate when compared to the average person. By contrast, in Jodo Shinshu Buddhism we accept the limitations of our ordinariness and seek to become who we are, without pretense, knowing that we are embraced just as we are. Honen, Shinran's teacher and the founder of the Jodo Shu school of Pure Land Buddhism, put it succinctly: "In the Path of Sages one perfects wisdom and achieves enlightenment: in the Path of Pure Land one returns to the foolish self to be saved by Amida."

This "foolish self" is called "bombu" in Japanese. It is who we all are. While we can be said, in the ultimate sense, to have buddha-nature, in a much more immediate and everyday sense we have bombu-nature. Noting our bombuness means recognizing our imperfection, our limitations, with an air of chagrin but also acceptance. Our bombuness is the source of much humour in the Jodo Shinshu tradition.

To be foolish is normal. Our heroes and opponents all share in this foolishness. We discover our foolish nature by the shining light of Amida Buddha, the light of wisdom, which reveals our shortcomings. It's hard for a fool to recognize their own foolishness, which is why we rely on power-beyond-self. Some traditions of Buddhism rely on supposedly enlightened masters or reincarnated saints. But time and again, scandals over sex, money, and power reveal them to be fools like the rest of us under their fancy robes. Therefore, we turn toward Amida Buddha, wisdom beyond the human, to show us our limitations (and without taking advantage of them).

Dr. Mark Unno, a professor of Japanese Buddhism and Jodo Shinshu minister, told a story at the New York Buddhist Church one time that has stuck with me because of how well it illustrates bombuness. Dr. Unno was invited to a weekend seminar. He rented a red Thunderbird, an eye-catching, souped-up vehicle, and proudly drove his family down the California coast. Although the light was dim outside, the other cars he passed didn't have their headlights on. He was stunned at this carelessness; it made him feel that he was an especially good driver, since he alone was responsible and drove with his headlights shining brightly. As he drove on, telling himself how good he was and beginning to suspect that the other drivers were suffering brain damage due to air pollution, he finally couldn't contain his pride any further. He started boasting about using his headlights and belittling the other drivers around him, showing off to his passengers. His cousin replied, "You know, you can take your sunglasses off now."

The most common format for Dharma talks in North American and Hawaiian Jodo Shinshu temples is a greeting, followed by a story from the minister's life about some foolish thing they did, and then application of the Dharma to reveal the more universal lesson that can be drawn from this embarrassing or unfortunate incident. By refusing to be a sage, a spiritual icon higher and holier than others, the minister reveals their bombuness and invites the sangha to reflect on their own bombu nature.

This insistence on our common foolishness is a resource for dealing with conflict. Conflict with others is inevitable: it is especially common when working to bring about needed change in the world. When conflict occurs, it's natural for us to become self-protective. We automatically assume that we (our side) are right, and they (the other side) are wrong. Because today's media environment rewards polarization and extremism, this tendency can be magnified a hundredfold, quickly causing people (regardless of what position they take) to see those who disagree as not simply different, or even wrong, but actually evil and dangerous. We are rapidly losing the skill of disagreeing without hate, because the systems we are trapped in do not sufficiently reward reasonableness or consensus. The middle path is anathema to current politics, social media, and tribalism.

And yet, no matter how strongly right we feel (or how strongly we feel they are wrong), both sides are bombus. Nearly twenty years ago, I was on a panel for the Eastern Buddhist League with Dr. Taitetsu Unno, one of the most important Jodo Shinshu teachers of the 20th century. I don't remember what poor advice I gave about conflict resolution, but Dr. Unno's words have stayed with me ever since. When considering a conflict, he said, the most important point to always remember is that I am a source of the conflict. And the next most important point is to try to manifest the strength and wisdom provided by the Dharma to deal with my own subjective biases, and thus become more open to other people's views, whether or not I agree with them.

When Dr. Unno made these comments, I was really struck by them. At first, I didn't want to agree with him. I felt that in a conflict, someone should be right, and someone should be wrong. And that often it was the other person who was wrong, not me.

But as I reflected further, I came to see the deep wisdom in what he said. Conflict always involves two people. No matter how wrong I think someone is, there couldn't be a conflict with them unless I was there getting involved in the dispute. More to the point, if my ego wasn't there asserting itself as "right," there could not be a conflict. So, I am always a contributing factor to every conflict I encounter.

I may wish the other person to change to suit my whims, but in reality I am completely unable to change someone else's ego and attachments. But often I'm able to become more aware of my own negative contributions to each situation. Dr. Unno spoke about being strong and wise enough to deal with our own biases. But very importantly, he doesn't mean our own small, self-attached efforts at self-understanding. He means the strength and wisdom provided by the Dharma, by the light of Amida Buddha, which shines into the darkness of my bombu-nature and illuminates it for me. By encountering that wisdom-light, I am made aware of how I foolishly contribute to conflicts with others. Then I can begin to deal with others in a more humble, healthy manner. In this way, I begin to resolve conflicts in the spirit of Shinran's Buddhism.

Even in those times when I'm positive that I'm right, I can try to keep my ego from making a conflict worse than it is. And as I come to know my own attachment and delusion, I can develop sympathy and understanding for others who are also dealing with their own ego problems. No matter how entrenched our political or other differences become, they spring from the same source on both sides. All people want happiness and dislike suffering, and they ignorantly pursue these things to the best that they know how. Every person who disagrees with us is a bombu, like us. They too are foolish, fumbling creatures, flailing about in this difficult world. They cling to the wrong things and try fruitless methods of self-protection or opposition. They are like mirrors—in them I see the same bombuness that I too possess.

We still need to stand by our principles, to work for good as we understand it, and oppose forces that cause suffering. Conflict will never be avoidable. But it is best if we can enter the fray with a clear understanding that all involved are bombus. Our ultimate goal is to live in the Pure Land together with all beings—that means those who agree with us and those who oppose us. My direst enemy is embraced just as greatly as I am by Great Compassion. That's crucial to keep in mind when involved in the challenging, upsetting, sometimes dangerous work of pushing for a more just, inclusive, and environmentally sustainable society.

Deep Listening/Receiving

In many forms of Buddhism, the metaphor for practice and awakening is one of sight. People talk about seeing the truth, seeing things as they really are, and so on. This sort of metaphor is relatively assertive: one reaches out via one's own efforts and seizes/penetrates/masters the truth hidden from us. Meditation is described as seeing, as observing one's thoughts, despite meditation often lacking an actual visual component. The assertive quality comes through because our intuitive sense of sight is that it is a faculty that goes out from the eye and contacts the world (even though that's not how it operates biologically). The assertiveness of sight is clear in the way we feel uncomfortable when we have a sense that someone is watching us—we don't have the same anxieties that someone we haven't detected might be smelling or hearing us.

The Path of the Pure Land, on the other hand, uses the metaphor of *receiving* the truth, through the faculty of deep listening. Hearing is a passive sense: sounds come to us, and we receive them. It's so engrained in our approach that Shinran even refers to the sense of hearing when he discusses the light of Amida:

> The light shines everywhere, ceaselessly;
> Thus Amida is called "Buddha of Uninterrupted Light."
> Because beings hear this power of light,
> Their mindfulness endures and they attain birth
> [in the Pure Land].

This is our method of practice: deeply listening, turning our bodies and hearts in the direction that Great Compassion's light is shining on us, so that we receive the light and are nourished by it. As practitioners we are like plants, flourishing in the power of the light. Nurtured by the light, we are empowered and can generate fruits of compassion for others to receive.

So deep is this sense of receiving that we don't even claim the nembutsu that spills from our lips. In Jodo Shinshu it is taught that when we are saying the nembutsu, it is Amida Buddha calling us. The sound of our voices is the sound of the Buddha's voice, calling us to listen, as Rev. Kenryu Tsuji notes in a hymn:

> When I call Amida's Name
> It's Amida calling me;
> Buddha's voice, my voice are one.
> I gassho to Amida.

When we listen deeply, we find that everything is constantly teaching the Dharma to us. This is the meaning of the flowers, trees, wind, birds, and other phenomena of the Pure Land preaching the Dharma. Everything becomes nembutsu, in this shared sangha of Boundless Life. As Rev. Tsuji says in a poem:

> The Nembutsu is the sound of the universe.
> It is the sound of the wind as it rustles the leaves;

It is the roar of the waves as they rush toward the shore;
It is the song of the robin, the whippoorwill
and the chorus of cicadas on a summer evening.
The Nembutsu is naturalness....

With the mind of receiving, we can listen deeply to what the world is teaching us. We can listen to hear the cries of those who suffer and seek to understand the sources of their pain. We can listen to the groans of the Earth and seek to perceive how we are harming it. We can listen to the anger of our opponents and seek to find our inner togetherness so that we don't lose sight of their humanity even as we work in opposition. A receiving attitude cuts down on our arrogance and egocentricity, allowing new possibilities to come to us and transform our actions.

Mappo (DharmaFail)

Anyone who pays even the slightest bit of attention to the news is aware that the world is sliding into disaster. Our natural, political, social, economic, and all other systems are under tremendous stress and are increasingly non-functional. Human activities have created multiple environmental crises, from rapid warming to species extinction. Borders strain with refugees fleeing violence, poverty, climate disasters, and more.

None of this is news to Pure Land Buddhists. Jodo Shinshu emerged from a time of profound crisis—it was made for times precisely like these. In Buddhism it is understood that the teaching and practice of the Dharma declines over time, and that in tandem the world degenerates too. There is a period after the death of a Buddha when the teachings are well-preserved and the established practices are still effective. This is the period of the Right Dharma. Over time, Buddhism becomes bloated, monks pursue prestige and comfort more than service and awakening, and it becomes extremely difficult to truly walk the path and reach Buddhahood. This is the period of the Semblance Dharma. As people stray from following the Dharma, greed and anger spread, and world conditions worsen. As the social and natural world deteriorate, conditions for practicing the Dharma become even worse, as the cycle feeds on itself.

Ultimately, the world enters the Final Age of the Dharma, called Mappo in Japanese. This is the age of DharmaFail, when Buddhism is falling apart and precious teachings are being lost. As conditions deteriorate and people's hearts weaken, old practices become ineffectual and complete awakening during this lifetime is impossible. Forms remain as mere shells; monks wear robes and expect respect but do little to truly earn it. Meanwhile, the world experiences disaster after disaster, as war, storms, epidemics, famine, and other crises become the norm. Caught in a worsening world and with the shelter of Buddhism so tattered that it no longer provides effective refuge, ordinary people experience terrible suffering. At the end of this long period Buddhism falls apart completely, and the Dharma is lost for a long time until another Buddha awakens to restart the cycle by once again showing the way to liberation.

In Shinran's lifetime, Buddhists in East Asia understood that they were far removed from the time of the Buddha and had entered Mappo. Shinran and his teacher Honen looked at the state of Buddhism, the constant wars of Japan, and the terrible suffering of the masses. They knew that Mappo was closing in around them and only radical solutions would suffice.

Thankfully, the Buddha didn't leave us bereft, even in this troubled age so far from his own. In the *Larger Pure Land Sutra* the Buddha predicted that the Pure Land teachings would be the very last ones to die out, because they were specially designed for those of us in the age of DharmaFail. Drawing on the power of Shakyamuni Buddha's teachings about Amida Buddha, Shinran and his colleagues spread the message of hope and universal liberation throughout medieval Japan. Because it was so suited to the times and the people stuck in them, Pure Land grew to be extremely influential in Japan.

Eight hundred years later, we are even deeper into the age of DharmaFail. When we look around, we can plainly see that the old ways do not work. Famous teachers commit scandal after scandal, and even meditation becomes a commodity for the rich to indulge in on pricey retreats, while the rest of us desperately cling to smart phone apps or self-help books to try and achieve some mindfulness amidst our struggles. As the climate heats, the seas rise, species die out, democracy teeters, and hate spreads, the people's Buddhism of the Pure Land way becomes ever more relevant, just as the Buddha predicted. We aren't happy about the current situation, but it's hardly a surprise. We've known about DharmaFail for generations and are already prepared to deal with it.

Climate change is a dramatic and scary process, and many things are lost along the way, but there is life on the other side. Maybe human, maybe not. Any given species may or may not make it. But there is life, and wherever there is life there will once again be diversity. As a child of the Cold War era, I firmly believed that I and all living things would perish in a nuclear war. I believed *all* things were already lost, we were just waiting for the single moment when the bombs would actually fall, and that foregone conclusion would be reached. I never expected to live out my natural lifespan; I never expected to reach adulthood. But here I am, and here we are, so many living things, still persisting. Now I see that so much can be *saved*. Awful as it is, I will take the climate crisis over nuclear war a thousand times and gladly.

At its root, in the age of DharmaFail we have a crisis of blind passions, of greed, anger, and ignorance, of selfishness and self-righteousness, of failed compassion and wisdom, which produce the ever-evolving damage we do to each other and the world around us. Without attacking the sources of greed, anger, and ignorance, we will never succeed in making substantive progress on mitigating climate change. To call it a climate emergency is imperfect because it suggests the problem is with the climate, when the problem is with ourselves, the human race. The climate crisis is merely one of a thousand effects of this cause.

In Jodo Shinshu metaphor, the ocean receives all the polluted rivers and purifies them. This represents the enormous power of Amida Buddha to take in all our polluted mental streams full of blind passions and transmute them into wisdom and compassion. It also helps me to see how the Earth's oceans operate. The ocean and the Earth do indeed have vast healing, purifying, and regenerative properties. In time they can purify anything we put into them, anything at all. There is no poison so vile, just as there is no bombu so evil, that they can't embrace and purify. However, they work on a larger and longer timescale than human beings, who are hectic and short-sighted. To allow those vast healing properties to best do their work, we need to slow down the production of yet more pollution, just as we need to avoid committing more evil just because we will be embraced. We need to work together with the ocean and Earth, doing our part as interdependent beings in the Sangha of Boundless Life. We need to reign in the destructive greed of corporations and the ultra-wealthy with their out-sized contributions to climate change and environmental destruction, and make changes in our own ordinary lifestyles that collectively contribute to local and global harm.

As we let the polluted streams of our hearts be cleansed by the power of Amida Buddha, and work to slow our own and others' destructive actions so the purifying work of the Earth can take place, we can let the inexhaustible support of Great Compassion buoy us in this time of despair. We can be thankful that this last great teaching of the Buddha was preserved and passed down to us amidst great difficulty so that it would be available to us now in this dreadful age. We can be grateful for what we're able to save and mourn those things that we lose. And we can take the long view: DharmaFail began before us and won't end until long after us. We're in this for the long haul, together. The only way we will survive is solidarity.

Inner Togetherness / *Kyosei* (Born Together) / *Ondobo Ondogyo*

Kaneko Daiei was a professor at the Jodo Shinshu university Otani Daigaku. Occasionally in his writings Kaneko used the term inner togetherness, by which he meant the natural bonds that we share with other beings. There is an emotional quality to this feeling of "fellowness" with others, so that when someone else is suffering, we too suffer. Troubled by the suffering of ourselves and others, we look to see what its cause is. We look at the real situations of actual people in their everyday lives, rather than focusing on the ideal of how we ought to be to avoid suffering. This is very much a Jodo

Shinshu path, as it looks to ordinary beings instead of abstractions.

There is a poem by the monk Ryokan that expresses this process very well:

When I think
About the misery
Of those in this world
Their sadness
Becomes mine.

Oh, that my monk's robe
Were wide enough
To gather up all
The suffering people
In this floating world.

Nothing makes me
More happy than
Amida Buddha's Vow
To save
Everyone.

Kaneko indicates that in realizing that we and others are fellow beings bonded by an inseparable inner togetherness, we seek a solution to our misery that will be adequate for all. The answer, according to Kaneko, is the Primal Vow of Amida Buddha, which embraces all beings just as they are and provides the nembutsu as the easy practice for liberation that anyone can perform.

This is about as far as Kaneko took his idea. I want to expand on the trail that he pointed out, fleshing out this concept of inner togetherness. As I understand it, inner togetherness arises from the fact of inter-relatedness. Inter-relatedness or interdependence is the central insight of Mahayana Buddhism. It means that nothing exists separate from all the other things in the universe. Every person lives only because they rely on the support of others. No matter how far out you trace the web of relations, there is always more that can be said about it: it is infinite and total, and only a

Buddha can truly perceive its full extent. Indeed, in the Mahayana tradition it is often said that comprehension of this totality is what provokes buddhahood or is buddhahood itself. Thus, while I seem in my deluded mind to be one individual person struggling in the world against others, in fact, from the Buddha's viewpoint, there is no separation between self and other. In traditional language this is often called emptiness, because we are empty of independent existence. But inner togetherness is a uniquely Jodo Shinshu term for this understanding, which stresses the positive side of connection and the fellowship aspect of the Pure Land way, without losing sight of the inseparable inter-relatedness that informs the basic concept.

So, there is no separation between self and other, and my life only exists because of others. It is the power of others, the power-beyond-myself, that sustains my entire existence. In Buddhism we talk about no-self, but another way to express it would be that when you have a near death experience, the entire history of the universe ought to flash before your eyes, because it is all—all of it—your own history. You and I and each person is the sum total of everything that has happened and is happening.

This vision of unshakable inner togetherness is embedded in our wish to be born together with all beings in the Pure Land. We seek a common destination that will be acceptable to all and accepting of all people. In this life, we have separations and disputes with other people based on our deluded egos: this is a fact of living that we cannot fully overcome. The story of the Pure Land upholds our greatest values: that even though we are imperfect, we are embraced by Great Compassion, and even though we aren't always able to get along now, our goal is total reconciliation and togetherness.

Shinran expressed this well in *Tannisho*, when he contrasted the Pure Land path with that of the sages. He said that the path of sages is to have pity and look down on other beings. Sages are great Buddhist saints who by their own efforts at meditation, ascetic practices, and so on have achieved freedom. But because they have separated themselves to reach freedom, they can't feel the pains of ordinary beings: they look down with pity upon the rest of us. The path of the Pure Land, by contrast, is to be born together with other beings into nirvana, the Pure Land, and then to immediately return to help others forever and ever. This Pure Land type of compassion keeps the practitioner in constant relationship to others, not separating oneself into a saint. If you become a saint, you are different from suffering beings and can no longer relate. Thus, from Shinran's perspective the arrogance of the saint represents a type of failure.

There is a story in the *Kudensho* that reflects Shinran's spirit well. In it, Shinran said that if someone loses a loved one and comes to you in distress, you shouldn't get on your high horse and tell them that Buddhism is about non-attachment, everyone dies, etc. Instead, Shinran said that you should briefly share the Dharma with them, then get them drunk. So, you drink with them, and when they can smile and forget their pain for a little while, you leave them be. Now, I don't know if this is the best answer or not, and the story may not be true, but it points to the feeling of Jodo Shinshu. You don't deliver some sort of abstract lesson about how all things arise and pass away and so people shouldn't be attached to anything; you just get right down there with the suffering person and share in their sorrow, drinking together and cheering them through your companionship. This is acting out of the recognition of inner togetherness, a recognition that brings you toward others rather than removing you from the everyday world.

In exploring this subject, we need to emphasize that being born with all beings is an attitude that is quintessentially Mahayana in orientation. The Pure Land is an expression of compassion, not selfishness. We seek the Pure Land because it is the place where we can be reconciled with everyone, not merely for our own individual liberation. There is no such thing as individual liberation: like Dharmakara Bodhisattva, who vowed never to achieve Buddhahood unless all beings would be liberated through the power of the nembutsu, we can't achieve Buddhahood unless all others are included in it.

Thus, I find that there's an emotional quality to the path of awakening in Jodo Shinshu which is very interesting. Shinran points to this heart feeling when he wrote to a follower in one of his letters, "Signs of long years of saying the nembutsu and aspiring for birth can be seen in the change in the heart that had been bad and in the deep warmth for friends and fellow-practitioners." Deep warmth for others is the sign of nembutsu coming to fruition in one's life, not detachment.

There's a story about Shoma, one of the wondrous Jodo Shinshu practitioners known as *myokonin*, which illustrates this well. Shoma walks into a temple and lays down in front of the inner shrine area. Everyone is shocked and they demand to know why Shoma feels emboldened to be so disrespectful. But Shoma replies that Amida is his loving parent and that he is like a silly child. He feels completely at home in the temple, as if he were in his own house. For a deeply awakened ordinary person like Shoma, there is an emotional warmth to his trusting, and there is no separation between the foolish being and buddha.

Inner togetherness is also a vision of totalness: all beings will be born together; all are embraced. In the *Kyogyoshinsho*, Shinran quotes the *Nirvana Sutra* as follows: "All sentient beings without fail ultimately realize great shinjin [awakening]." This vision of Shinran's was so expansive that elsewhere in the *Kyogyoshinsho*, Shinran says that 10 billion *maras* (these are the Buddhist equivalents of devils) were liberated when the *Moon Matrix Sutra* was preached, and that in the *Sun Matrix Sutra* the king mara (Satan himself, more or less, though the Buddhist concept differs from the Abrahamic one) was converted to Buddhism and worshipped the Buddha. That's an incredible concept. No other religion says that even the devil will become a buddha or saint. If even Mara will be liberated, that means that all beings, even those we hate, will be freed. And it means that even the aspects of ourselves that we hate the most will nonetheless be released in the end. Shinran doesn't even stop there, however. In *Notes on Essentials of Faith Alone*, Shinran proclaims that "Buddha-nature is none other than Tathagata. This Tathagata pervades the countless worlds; it fills the hearts and minds of the ocean of all beings. Thus, plants, trees, and land all attain Buddhahood."

When so much effort is spent in other religions dividing the world into the saved and the damned and proclaiming how other people are justifiable objects of our suspicion and even hate, this is an amazing, radical teaching. It can also be an uncomfortable one, because we are so used to having our prejudices confirmed for ourselves. If you take a moment to think of two or three people you dislike, you'll see what I mean. Perhaps it's a co-worker, or a politician, or a neighbor, or a media figure, or even a family member. Well, the Jodo Shinshu teaching says that that person is valued just as much as you, and they too are destined for the Pure Land. You can't get away from them.

That's good. As much as we may hate how unfairly others treat us, togetherness is the only way. Like the two-headed bird, we can't reject the other without harming ourselves. Every one of us bombus is a suffering being, and every one of us will continue to suffer as long as anyone suffers. In this failing world, we need to accept Amida Buddha's vision of mutual support among equals, and harmony between people and environment. We need to nurture every flower of the Pure Land and respect one another's beauty. We need to listen deeply to the teachings that we are receiving from air, water, creature, and community. We need to embrace all those who suffer and allow the flow of Great Compassion to circulate through us and beyond us. With sleeves rolled up, arms interlocked with one another, we need to pour forth from the Pure Land to help heal the world, supported by the Primal Vow.

Today, Shinran's way has become acceptable, and thus we may lose sight of the strong challenge he issued to his society. He was not a person of comfort and respectability—he was a person of the margins, persecuted and rejected, yet unwavering in his convictions even in the face of oppression. He is best understood as a minority figure outside of the acceptable, yet whose influence became so great that the borders of acceptability were eventually expanded in seemingly permanent fashion. To those who struggle today with our current status quos—be they related to norms of sexuality and gender, economics and class, race and ethnicity, environmental unsustainability, or other sources of suffering—Shinran is proof that change is possible within Buddhism and within society at large. Indeed, as Shinran's legacy demonstrates, the margins can become the mainstream. And when we become a Dharma radical like Shinran, we honour his legacy and keep his spirit alive.

Printed in the USA
CPSIA information can be obtained
at www.ICGtesting.com
LVHW041042150324
774367LV00006B/1122

9 781896 559902